# CYCLING TO THE

On December 27, 2013, Maria Leijerstam made history by becoming the first person in the world to cycle to the South Pole from the edge of the Antarctic continent. Simultaneously, she set a second world record for the fastest human-powered coast-to-South Pole traverse, completing her journey in 10 days, 14 hours, and 56 minutes.

Dedicated to this double world record, Maria spent four years meticulously planning, training, and preparing. She overcame daunting mental and physical challenges and assembled a winning team to accomplish what many thought impossible.

Before her Antarctic expedition, Maria had already established herself as a serious endurance athlete. In 2007, she became the first Welsh woman to complete the gruelling Marathon Des Sables, running six marathons across the Sahara Desert in seven days. In 2012, she was the first woman to finish the Siberian Black Ice Race, a 650-kilometre cycle across Lake Baikal (it was so dangerous that the race was run once and never again). She has also represented Great Britain on the World Series Adventure Racing circuit.

Maria's career began in rocket science with BAE Systems before transitioning to project management roles at various multinational companies, including Ford of Europe. In 2010, she merged her passion for sport with her business expertise by founding Multisport Ltd, an adventure sports company in Wales, UK. Through her company, she now hosts the successful Burn Series Adventure Races to introduce sport as a way of life to families and experienced athletes.

In addition to her professional and athletic endeavours, Maria is deeply rooted in her community and family life, managing the family deer farm and raising two daughters. Her multifaceted life is a testament to her belief in the power of determination, the importance of work-life balance, and the value of instilling a sense of adventure and resilience in the next generation.

# CYCLING TO THE SOUTH POLE

a world first

## MARIA LEIJERSTAM

10th Anniversary Edition

*Maria Leijerstam*

Foreword by

SIR RANUPLH FIENNES

First published in the UK in October 2017 by Profile Publishing

Second edition published in the UK in April 2024

Cycling to the South Pole

ISBN 979-8-88461-760-5

To my mother,

The kindest person I know.
Thank you for your dedication and patience in
helping me write my story.

# Contents

# Foreword

## by

# SIR RANULPH FIENNES

Every world record is a tremendous achievement, but this one demands a special place in polar history.

Maria is the first person to cycle to the South Pole from the edge of Antarctica, and she completed her expedition in the fastest human-powered recorded time. Her uniquely designed cycle demonstrates that cycling in Antarctica is a proven and achievable form of travel.

Pursuing a seemingly impossible goal that no one has achieved before and setting a record hugely energises our body and mind. The unobtainable works like an addiction. It powers you on your journey, and as a worldwide adventurer and explorer, I know from experience how goal setting is the essential fuel for any journey.

Maria started with no more than a childhood dream and describes herself as 'an ordinary woman.' Yet, through determination and smart expedition planning by Maria herself, she achieved two polar records.

I invite you to share with Maria the highlights and lowlights in this fantastic story of human endeavour—the body-stabbing 40 mph wind that threatens to whip her cycle into a crevasse, her determination to cycle every revolution of the way up the steep Leverett Glacier, and her day-to-day survival under the most severe conditions on Earth inside her tiny red tent.

This book will take the reader through undiscovered terrain but also remind you that you don't have to climb a mountain or traverse a glacier to realise your goal. Anyone who is faced with any challenge, however big, however small will find Maria's determination and will to succeed inspiring and relevant.

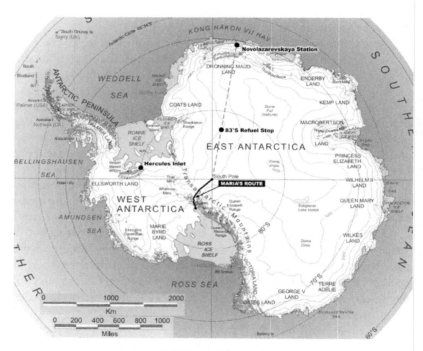

Image courtesy of NASA Image Collection / Alamy Stock Photo

# 1. Spinning My Globe – Where is Antarctica?

## "Look beyond possibility"

I can't believe it; I'm almost there. I've been cycling for 17 hours and can just make out the top of the glacier. I am struggling to control my mind, but it is trying to control me. Body and mind seem to be operating in a different sphere, and I am battling to calm the argument between them.

I imagine the stress on my leg muscles and feel the blood rushing through my veins as I pump the pedals in endless rotation. What will snap first: my thigh ligaments, my cycle chain or my mind?

I am cycling through a whiteout and can hardly see further than my handlebars. The icy incline is getting steeper and steeper, and my legs are weakening. High above me, I catch a glimpse of the menacing Transantarctic Mountain tops as they pierce the solid blanket of snow, filling me with horror. It's much worse—much, much worse than I'd expected. I fear I'm not going to make it to the top of the glacier. The blinding snow is swirling all around me, and at times, the gale-force winds momentarily lift my wheels. I know there are crevasses in this area. I'm petrified.

Suddenly, my rear wheel jars unexpectedly. I try to control my body and brace against the jolt, but I lose balance and slide off my seat, hitting the ice bottom first. Sprawling on a narrow ledge, my body seems uncontrollably numb, and my arms and legs refuse to gather strength. I stare down the steep, icy incline I have just cycled up. My

1

cries don't help, and I watch helplessly as my cycle rumbles away from me, tossing itself uncontrollably from side to side. It limps momentarily across a protruding snowy crust. "Please stop, please stop!" I scream. It does not stop but bumps down the steep, icy glacier, out of my sight into the whiteness.

As I struggle to my feet, I catch the outline of a dark, cylindrical shape in the snow just a couple of metres away. It might be my tent bag. I am praying it is my tent. Please let it be my tent. The gale is puncturing every part of my body, and my only hope is to take shelter. I am not ready to die. With my energy drained, I am unable to put one foot in front of the other. They are heavy with fatigue and refuse to respond to my efforts. I am reduced to crawling on all fours towards the bag shape, which seems further away than I thought. The incline is ridged with icy mounds that cut through the protection of my polar trousers, searing into my knees and shins. My whole body is shaking… I wake up with a jolt in a heavy sweat.

My bedclothes are sticky and uncomfortable. I feel drained by the poignant reality of this recurrent nightmare, which interrupts my nights in the year leading up to my expedition. How can a nightmare feel so real and wear me out mentally and physically before I even start the day, or for that matter, get out of bed?

I turn to my boyfriend Wayne for comfort. He is getting used to my nightmares disturbing his sleep. "I've got you," he said. But I feel horribly alone, especially at night, after such a graphic dream. I am setting myself what appears to everyone else to be an unobtainable target. During daylight hours, I am pumped up with excitement as I train and plan for every possible adversity on my journey to become the first person in the world to cycle to the South Pole. Yet all my preparation and determination collapse at night like a pack of cards. Was that dark shape on the ice my tent? Do I live or die? My nightmare always ends at the same point. I never have the answer.

I cannot sleep. Something inside seems to be telling me it is too dangerous to sleep. I may uncover something in my dream that will prevent me from reaching the South Pole. I cannot allow this to happen. I need to stay strong and not doubt myself. I force my mind to replace fear with rational thought as I repeatedly tell myself I am doing everything humanely possible to make my expedition successful.

I had an idyllic childhood, having been brought up on a picturesque hilltop farm in South Wales, where I was enveloped in the beauty and tranquil delights of nature. My closest companions were our turkeys, chickens and goats and Candy, my cherished dapple-grey pony, who stood eleven hands tall.

My best human friend was a boy named Nicky, who, like me, was half-Swedish. We met sitting in a sandpit at a playgroup, shovelling sand over each other and chatting away in Swedish—which was entirely natural as it was our first language.

I felt very close to Nicky, and hand in hand, we started school together. Looking back, he was like a brother, but we were very different. I remember to this day, Nicky would always eat the food he liked first, leaving to last what he disliked. This meant he had to sit at the table for what seemed to me like hours while he reluctantly finished the remainder of his food. I decided to eat what I disliked first, leaving the best bits to last, with the bonus of leaving the table in super-fast time. I wondered if this now shaped the way I made decisions— tackling challenges head-on with an understanding of type two fun—it may not be fun at the moment, but afterwards, you can look back and appreciate why you did it.

At the age of seven, my world turned upside down when Nicky's parents whisked him away to live in Usk, about 40 miles from our farm. Apart from meeting only occasionally after their move, I was most distraught by the fact that Nicky was given a large red box of Maltesers from our primary school as a leaving present. When I left, two years later, I was given a book on Princess Diana!

On my ninth birthday, my parents bought me a globe that I became secretly obsessed with. I placed it on my bedside table so I could spin it with my hand as I reached out from under the covers every night. My parents had shown me where we lived and where my grandmother lived in Sweden. It fascinated me. I spent every night spinning my globe, looking and learning about the size and location of the countries. I was frustrated that I could not see the extent of the big white continent at the bottom, which was masked by the stem that attached the globe to its base. Was this another country?

My parents were inspirational people. In addition to their day jobs, they worked tirelessly every evening and weekend to renovate our dilapidated old farmhouse, which they had bought when my sister was just six months old. I came into the world two and a half years later.

Our farmyard and fields were my playground, and there never seemed to be a dull moment. I would drag my sister Nina along on secret adventures down the steep incline at the back of the farm. I would swing on branches and leap across the fast-moving river below. Nina constantly challenged me to go first, and I thrived on her trust. Depending on the outcome of my escapade, she would follow suit. On the occasions when I skinned my shins or fell awkwardly, she stood back reluctantly.

She was the smarter of the two of us, and she proved it too, by getting higher marks than I did at school. I challenged her talents by insisting that I would become an astronaut or a polar explorer. It was my way of demonstrating I could be just as good as her.

I struggled with lessons at school. However hard I worked, I did not seem to achieve good results. I felt deeply disappointed upon receiving my GCSE results letter from my secondary school in Cowbridge, Vale of Glamorgan, which showed that I had received mostly Cs and Ds.

The only subject I really enjoyed was Mathematics. The pleasure of solving a problem or working out an equation gave me great satisfaction and left me with the desire for more. This was due partly to my cheerful Maths teacher. He had a great sense of humour and made solving even the most difficult fraction fun. He called top heavy fractions 'Dolly Partons', and his definition of infinity was a number 'almost as old as the French teacher!' I wanted to study Mathematics A-level but could not translate my passion into good exam results.

I have a vivid recollection of a particular day in my English class. I was thirteen years old and carried a helping of the self-consciousness that besets many teenagers. I particularly dreaded drawing attention to myself in class. It was my turn to read a passage aloud.

As I rose to my feet, I took in the fine details of the austere Victorian classroom: twigs that crows had dropped down the chimney into the fireplace in the corner, the peeling varnish on the high vaulted wooden ceiling and the outside chill from the draughty windows. Oh, I so wished I could be outside.

All eyes in the room were on me, and I started, in a trembling whisper, to read a passage from an article about farming. The word 'fertilise' approached like a formidable barrier, and I stumbled, my tongue betraying me with 'fertilisation.'

The class erupted into raucous laughter. The echo bounced off the walls as if the whole building was laughing at me. My teacher's face turned a shade of crimson that matched my blushing, and he pointed a rigid finger toward the door, his voice booming with the command to leave. I looked over to one of my friends, who turned the other way, and then, in floods of tears, stood in the corridor and reflected on the pieces of my shattered confidence as other children walked past, smirking at my predicament. Since that day, my fear of reading aloud was crippled to the point that my kind friend Anne Katherine would sit beside me and quietly whisper in my ear the passage I had to read in advance.

When, towards the end of my time at school, my teachers suggested I give up on education, it angered me and made me even more determined to struggle on.

In 1996, with disappointing A-level results, my mother and I headed off to Plymouth University to beg for a place on the mathematics degree course. I was impressed that the university was not dismissive of my poor grades but was keen to encourage me. When an acceptance letter finally arrived in the post, I was delighted. My persistence had paid off.

It was when I joined the Officer Training Corps at university that my thirst for adventure really took hold. Apart from the exciting-looking videos and pictures of military activities and adventure sports, an enticing addition was the gin and tonic that could be bought for only 40p in the officer's mess bar in Exeter.

Entry into the organisation was tough, with three days of physical and mental testing, demoralisation and character analysis. We were woken at unearthly hours and told to run up a hill or complete an assault course. I had never heard so much yelling from a sergeant in my life. I was shocked at his language and nervous about his aggressive demands, but there was little time to reflect; we just had to get on with it. We were given military missions with masses of different variables, which my logical mathematical brain enjoyed. I managed to replace my initial discomfort with determination because the result, like solving a Maths problem, brought me great satisfaction.

I passed the selection, and during my university years, I spent every Wednesday afternoon and most weekends running around Woodbury Common, Dartmoor and in the barracks in Exeter, enjoying military training, adventure sports and drinking gins. I was being paid for enjoying myself. It couldn't get better! Here, I learnt some of the most valuable lessons in my life about friendship, teamwork and overcoming difficult situations. It made me a much rounder person and allowed me to see situations from multiple perspectives. Most importantly, it fuelled my desire for adventure and exploring—perhaps one day, I, too, could follow in the footsteps of famous explorers. But first, I had to earn a living.

By the end of my second year at university, a light flickered on in my brain, and I learnt how to learn. My Mathematics degree was my passport to the business world, and I settled into a post with BAE Systems, one of the world's largest aerospace and defence companies.

During four years at BAE Systems, I was among 25 graduates selected from thousands of applicants to have a place on the SIGMA scheme to groom the next generation of managing directors. I felt my success had less to do with my mathematical ability and more with my drive, commitment and common sense.

I was determined to excel. I replaced my long, blonde hair with a more sophisticated cut and my short skirts with modest suits as I began an explosive career, moving all over the world for six-to-twelve-month periods, holding various posts. Life was buzzing. I enjoyed my career but soon realised I was entrenched in a military world. I was not prepared to narrow my options.

If I was going to broaden my horizons, I needed to take a leap. I had learnt to live my life by the principles of the Sigmoid curve, an s-shaped mathematical function. The curve initially has a down phase during the learning phase as you find your feet. It then goes up during the growth phase before reaching the decline phase. The idea is to jump onto the next Sigmoid curve during the growth phase to continue your journey upwards.

I decided it was time to switch from corporate work to consultancy to see how businesses operated from a different perspective. More importantly, I wanted to explore other industries. During an interview with a project management consultancy in London, I decided not to correct the interviewer, who wrongly interpreted a sentence in my CV. It read 'three years on the Sigma scheme', but he interpreted it as 'I have three years' experience of Six Sigma.'

As soon as I received the offer letter from the project management agency to join them as a Six Sigma specialist at Ford of Europe in Cologne, I accepted without hesitation. I had little practical experience with the discipline, so I headed out to the nearest bookshop to buy myself a book on Six Sigma. I had two weeks before my start date to teach myself three years of experience on the subject!

During my ten years in the world of business, my love for adventure challenges grew. Most weekends were spent running across mountain tops, competing in triathlons, kayaking across some of England's finest lakes and climbing mountains and cliff faces in Scotland and the south coast of England. Most importantly, with a stable salary, I could save for what had become my secret dream of travelling to Antarctica.

I don't really know why I was so obsessed with Antarctica. It began with that tingle of excitement when, as a child, I first discovered the hidden continent at the base of my globe all those years ago. I also loved the cold. It's possible that my love for the cold was a trait passed down from my father. He used to take us on skiing trips to Sweden, where the winter snow transformed the landscape into a wondrous playground.

The cold invigorated me and lit sparks of excitement inside me. I soon learnt to weave neatly through the pine forests, much faster than my sister, and I was always the last to part with my skis, reluctantly at the end of the day.

Whatever the reason, I had a passion that was not going away. In my spare time, I absorbed all I could about Antarctica: its climate, the host of countries that had set up scientific projects there and, of course, its explorers. I wanted even more to be part of it.

I had been in a relationship for a few years with Will, whom I met in the Officer Training Corps at university. I developed much of my love for adventure in the outdoors from him. He was an incredible climber, cyclist and kayaker. We got along well, and finding someone on the same wavelength as me was great.

Most winter weekends, after we left our jobs on Friday evening, we packed the car full of climbing kit and made the long drive to Glencoe. Arriving at 3 am, we put our tent up in the field of the Clachaig Inn and snatched a few hours of sleep before daylight. We were too excited about our ice climb to be tired. Scotland's dramatic peaks provided a welcome refreshment from our day jobs. I was a beginner at climbing but Will taught me to be confident and sensible. Hammering in ice screws in the freezing cold was a true test of my trust in Will, and it was reciprocated when he encouraged me to go first. When I think back, it was a potluck game, climbing up slabs of vertical ice and frozen cascading waterfalls, perched halfway up a mountain, trying to assess if the slab was strong enough to take the screws. The thrill of the unknown, the adrenalin rush, and the cold always coaxed my mind back to Antarctica.

In 2008, during a 50-mile ultra race along the Thames path from Reading to Shepperton, I met a competitor who told me about adventure racing. "I reckon you would really love it. Best of all, it takes you to amazing places around the world," he said. I couldn't resist a quick Google search later that day. It brought up the SleepMonsters website, and in a matter of seconds, I was hooked on its compelling details about adventure racing.

Expedition adventure racing is a multi-day, multi-discipline, non-stop race that takes mixed teams of four across untrodden territory in some of the remotest parts of the world. The race involves running, cycling, kayaking and navigating, as well as a whole array of other sports at the organiser's discretion. It is still a young sport in the UK, but its variety enthralled me. The only female in the team is rather scathingly labelled as 'compulsory baggage' by some; strangely, I found this demotion enticing.

I joined the forum promptly. Before I knew it, I was signed up for my first expedition race in Ireland during the summer of 2008. It was one of twelve World Series races, so I really started at the top. I booked a week off work to put myself through 600 kilometres of non-stop running, cycling and kayaking with three teammates I barely knew.

This was the first time I experienced throbbing swollen foot syndrome, which feels like walking on thousands of needles with every footstep. Just keeping awake demands massive self-control and being physically active for many days and nights gnaws into your body. I learnt the effects of sleep deprivation, and I learnt about my body and mind in ways I didn't know possible. Hallucinations are common during sleepless adventure races, and on the third day, I had an experience I will never forget.

I was walking closely behind my teammate Tim, a swimming coach regularly placed at the top in Ironman triathlons. Tim was the fittest in our team, yet at this moment, his history was irrelevant. We walked in single file along an Irish mountain ridge at 3 am in the light of a half-moon. The temperature was in low single figures. The wind was beginning to gain strength. I was wrapped up warmly, yet Tim was gloveless and didn't have his hat on. I realised something was wrong when he began to weave uncontrollably from side to side. "Tim!" I shouted, grabbing hold of his backpack.

"Where am I?" Tim spluttered. He was white, shivering violently and incomprehensible. "Mona Lisa needs me," he continued.

"We need to warm him up and quickly!" warned Russ, my other teammate.

Without further discussion, we unpacked our survival pack, dumped our kit on the ground and began to climb inside. The pack was a simple sheet of material with no poles, so we sat under the sheet, placing our bottoms around the edge of the material with our heads supporting the top. Still holding onto Tim, I decided not to remove his rucksack as I knew every hint of warmth around him was essential. He slumped down in a heap in front of us and seemed to lose total control of his body. It was apparent Tim had early-onset hypothermia. We needed to get heat into him quickly. Without further thought, I took off my coat, pulled up my jumper, unzipped his jacket and shared my 37-degree body heat directly to where it mattered—his chest.

I gazed across at my other two teammates, slightly embarrassed but still with Tim pressed up against my chest. It felt odd, yet in the severity of the moment, it was absolutely the right thing to do to save his life. No comment was passed, and we remained intertwined until dawn broke. By then, Tim's strength was revived by the warmth our tightly pressed bodies had generated. It was all about survival. Three days later, we crossed the finish line with stories and experiences that I will never forget.

Career and adventure were beginning to clash. There were not enough hours in the day, so I decided to change jobs and work closer to home. Previously I had been offered a job with a multinational company specialising in office and manufacturing operations. I made a call to see if there were any vacancies in the UK. Much to my delight, there was an opening in Lean Six Sigma. I took the job immediately, and it wasn't long before I was promoted to Head of Business Improvement for the IT division in the UK. The challenge made me ooze with excitement.

It didn't last. A few months after joining the company, I realised I'd chosen a tough nut to crack. Being young, new, and female was a barrier in this traditional company. I worked day in and day out for eighteen months to make alliances around the business. For the first time in my life, I began to feel that I could not cope with the situation as my values and those of my business colleagues were oceans apart. There were barriers to my developing, learning and progressing, and I was rapidly slipping down the wrong side of my Sigmoid curve. At the same time, my life of adventure was taking hold, and I was not prepared to let the difficulties in my corporate life hold me back.

# 2. On the Wrong Side of Life

"Extreme exhaustion makes teamwork hard to master"

In the summer of 2009, I took a week off work to race in a team of four at the Adventure Racing World Championships in Portugal. I spoke to no one about my mounting work dilemmas; I just wanted to shut them away. I seemed to have an engine inside me that was firing on all cylinders, yet I had no release for all this energy. My mental strength was dwindling at work.

Would I be able to build it up again by testing my physical and mental abilities in a different environment?

The race started from the Castle of Lousa, Coimbra, and covered 900 kilometres on foot, bike, and kayak across the Portuguese Algarve. Top teams from all over the world were battling it out in the most brutal of races. I teamed up with adventure racers Paul, Chris, and Gary, and we set the realistic target of finishing the race rather than winning it.

We were out in the wilderness carrying loaded rucksacks and all our climbing kit, as well as our wetsuits for the canyoning section of the trek. We climbed a total of 10,000 metres—higher than Everest! I felt good and determined more than ever to complete the race. We climbed on hands and feet up steep banks and wound our way along narrow, rocky tracks, plunging through pools of ice-cold water.

Our team spirit was tested to the limit, and we began to fall out over our differing and dwindling energy levels. Gary was frustrated that I was slow on the mountain biking section. The air began to ooze with negative tension. Annoyed by Gary's impatience with my progress on the mountain biking, I retorted impatiently during the run section when he lagged. "Come on, keep up," I said. My lack of diplomacy didn't help. He never forgave me.

Disaster struck three days into the race when we had to pull out due to our slow progress. I was determined to continue, but because we were so behind, our only option was to cycle the whole way to the finish and miss out on the remaining checkpoints. For me, it was about reaching the end as a competitive team. The others felt differently. Paul announced the decision to pull out. I was devastated and broke down in tears.

The boys were quick to climb into the support van and fall asleep while I sat outside on my holdall for some time, trying to piece together what had happened. What could have changed our decision? Had we slept for an hour before deciding to pull out, would it have been different?

I gazed down at my dusty trainers and eased out my feet. My thin socks stuck to my skin with a mixture of sweat, dirt and blood. My big toe was throbbing, and my soles felt like I had just walked over a bed of hot coals. The pain was a required by-product of my drive and determination to succeed. As always, I filtered my initial distress by summoning up images of the amazing path I had trodden.

The terrain had been severe, dramatic and awe-inspiring. Rocky climbs with brief respites through quaint hilltop villages, rushing rivers to navigate and dense undergrowth that prickled and disguised our route. I was part of a fast-moving film that I was unable to pause. Yet all this mellowed into a blur as I realised my real battle lay ahead.

I had deflected my stress about work by putting myself through intense physical punishment, which I had trained my mind to cope with. My body would heal, but would my mind continue to be strong to tackle my workplace problems? After finding no answer, I, too, crawled into the van alongside the lads and fell asleep instantly.

My passion for adventure racing continued to flourish every weekend, allowing me to switch off from mounting work dilemmas. My rollercoaster rides at work during the week ended late on Friday evenings when I turned to ultra-physical challenges to bring me peace of mind.

The G4 Land Rover Challenge set my passion alight when I was chosen from over 60,000 applicants to attend a national selection at the Land Rover centre in Hertfordshire. The experience made the Officer Training Corps selection seem easy.

At the end of the weekend, we lined up, waiting for the results to be read out. Two men and two women were to be chosen to represent the United Kingdom in a three-week expedition across Mongolia. I couldn't bear the prospect of failure. When my name was read out as one of the winning women, I thought I would collapse with joy. It felt as though I had been rescued from all my work traumas, and to top it all, Victoria Pendleton, the G4 Land Rover ambassador, commented that the winning four were exceptional athletes, excelling in everything they had been tested in. I felt unstoppable.

My world had turned around, and I was much more bullish about coping with the stress of my job. I trained hard before and after work in preparation for the Mongolian trip and tried equally hard to rescue the difficult situation unfolding at work. Then, one day in December, I received a call from the G4 Land Rover team to say that the Mongolian expedition had been cancelled due to the economic crisis. I felt myself die inside.

I went home and tried to make light of the situation. It was hard. I lived alone in a flat in Teddington. I didn't really know anyone apart from work colleagues, and I was in an exceedingly frustrating job. Black clouds descended on my usually optimistic horizon.

The mornings were the worst. For the first ten seconds of waking, after a disturbed sleep, I drifted into a dreamy trance, but then a thunderbolt would hit me, and I felt a deep stabbing pain inside. I nagged myself to get out of bed, but as my feet touched the cold wooden floor in my bedroom, it felt like my soul was being ripped apart. I was shaking, crying and sweating. I was in a spiral of depression, and I could not see a way out. I seemed to be in a strait jacket serving a sentence. There was only one door to go through that led down the stairs, out through the front door into my car and to the office, where every minute of the day seemed out of my control.

The same depression seemed to permeate my evenings. I never got to know my neighbours. A punk rocker on the top floor and a grumpy couple in the basement were always putting notices on my car, saying I had parked in the wrong place. I signed up for a salsa class to meet like-minded people but didn't find anyone I could relate to. Everyone seemed happy and content in their worlds, and there was no space for me. I was desperate to find a companion—someone to hang out with, go to the cinema with or drop into a bar for a drink—more than that, I needed to share my problems. I needed someone who could advise me on what to do about work and how to control my growing depression. But my pride would not allow me to admit to myself and others that I had seemingly failed at my job. There seemed to be no way out.

I joined the triathlon club and sprinted around the athletic stadium to numb my nerves. Everything I did became depressing. In a final attempt to lift my spirits, I started to date my swimming instructor. Even he turned out to be a weirdo after I received a photo from him wearing my own swimming costume. What on earth was he thinking?

I caught a virus that weakened me totally. I was so rock bottom that my body was unable to fight it. I could not do anything for myself, and I was so grateful when my mother drove down from Wales to look after me.

As we sat side by side in the doctor's surgery, I nervously completed the questionnaire handed to me by the receptionist. It asked blatantly in black and white whether I had ever contemplated suicide. I had to admit that on a few occasions after returning from work, I'd propped open the sash window that looked out onto the road from my sitting room and sat precariously on the sill, wondering whether my life had really become so intolerable. As tears streamed down my face, I could barely see the road beneath. I'd lean a little, then a little more, taking one foot off the floor as I lent. I'd change position to try and become a little more unstable, but every time, my final response was to withdraw, fall back into the room and sob and sob.

I stole a glance at my mother and wondered, should I lie to protect her from worry, or is it now time for me to finally open up? "I've been asked if I've ever contemplated suicide," I mumbled weakly as I pointed to the question on the paper. As my mother leant over to read it, I ticked the box 'yes.' Her face contorted into a painful grimace as she grabbed hold of me and cuddled me hard.

"You're going to be okay. I'm here for you. We're going to get this sorted," she said.

I was diagnosed with depression and written off work by my doctor. For the next month, I rarely left my flat. Both physically and emotionally, I felt too weak to move. Initially, I was suspicious about my weekly visits to the psychiatrist, but as the visits progressed, for the first time in my life, I felt myself let go. I could tell her everything without worrying about being judged, and, most importantly, I wasn't judging myself. I needed to get better, and I needed to do this fast. Sometimes, I would cry so hard that I couldn't speak. She put no pressure on me, sitting quietly in an unassuming position as I worked my way through her box of tissues.

I talked in detail about every individual at work. Why did they upset me, and what did they do? I talked about my loneliness and my eerie flat that I hated. I spoke of my failed relationships and whether I'd done the right thing in breaking up with my last boyfriend, whom I was still very fond of. She never interrupted my ramblings, and very gradually, after many visits, I slowly climbed up the recovery ladder, one step at a time.

Four weeks on, I had a phone call from an adventure racing friend called Nicola. "There is a race in Durham tomorrow. I haven't seen you for ages. Why don't you come up?" I hesitated. The last thing I wanted to do was socialise with people, and I had done very little sport for the last few months. "I'm feeling a bit low right now," I admitted. Nicola ignored my feeble reply and started planning where we could meet up.

Without much thought, I pulled on my running leggings and started my car. I drove in a dream, but at least I had a purpose. It wasn't until I got close to Durham that I stopped the car to see if I had my trainers in the boot. Fortunately, I did, but on arrival, I found out it was a cycling race as well, and I hadn't bought my bike. Once again, Nicola ignored my total lack of preparation and urged me to take part in the running section of the race. 'I've got this far, so I really have to do it,' I told myself. Breathing in the cool air and feeling that competitive spirit start to surface once more was refreshing. For a short time, I brushed away my depression.

At registration, I met a tall, handsome guy called Wayne with a foreign accent, and after a half-hearted attempt at the running part of the race, I helped to marshal on the cycling sections. Wayne joined me and told me he owned the company hosting and sponsoring the race. It was the off-road running shoe company called INOV8. I gazed down at my Salomon trainers and tried feebly to hide my feet in the mud. "I do own some INOV8s and they are my favourite off-road running shoes. I wore them out after running the Original Mountain Marathon in Scotland," I told him, as I wondered why I was trying to impress him. He acknowledged my pathetic excuse and swiftly changed the subject.

I told him I was a freelance business improvement consultant and, half seriously, I said I could advise him on cost-saving measures. To my surprise, he responded. "Yes, that would be good. Why don't you write me a proposal?"

A few days later, I had a phone call to ask how my proposal was coming along. After some detailed study on Wayne's company and some frantic hours putting a proposal together in the evenings, we met over dinner to discuss my suggestions. After all my efforts, he hardly mentioned the proposal I had written. Clearly, he was not interested in my work; he was interested in me.

After one month's sick leave, I returned to work nervously. What would everyone think of me? As I walked back into the office, I wanted to be invisible. My head was pounding, and I felt sickened to the core as I gazed around at an existence I hated. I sat down at my desk by the window. 'I am not going to let myself turn into a quivering wreck again,' I said to myself.

I picked up the phone to call my boss's secretary to see if he could meet me that morning. She politely informed me that he had moved back to Germany and had no space in his diary for the next three weeks. I could handle my frustration no longer. I made an instant decision with no thought of the consequences. I stood up from my desk, looked around the office at my colleagues, bowed over their computers and walked straight out. I was leaving with immediate effect.

Liberation at last! I decided that I would never go back to rising at 6 a.m. to don a suit and speed down the M3 to reach the office, and I decided that I would not follow procedures and processes that I felt were wrong. The buzz of the corporate world evaporated. I was 32 years old and unemployed. I returned my company car, gave up my flat in London, and went home to live with my parents in South Wales.

Strangely, after the initial shock of my resignation, my new situation excited me. Now, I could live by one of my most important values—the freedom to follow my instincts. In the past, I had tended to measure my success in terms of career, salary, home, the type of car I drove, and, to a certain extent, what I thought was expected of me. Now, it was all about what my instinct was telling me. It was poles apart from what my corporate life had taught me, where everything needed to be measured and traceable. My instinct provided freedom, excitement, and a chance to open the door to new opportunities.

# 3. New Zealand - Land of Adventure

"Being happy is the only true measure of success"

The thunderous clouds that had ruled my days at work were clearing, and I could hardly believe that I had allowed them to obscure my view for so long. With the loss of my comfortable salary, my lifestyle was back to basics.

Wayne's business commitments meant he was tied either to his head office in Durham or to flying around the world on business trips. I was floundering in South Wales, trying to shape a new future and work out how to combine my love of adventure with my business experience to earn a living.

We were not a couple, but we kept in regular contact on Skype, where we seemed to discuss more personal things rather than business. Maybe one day, it would lead to something more. I still had bouts of feeling unsettled, confused and unsure of where my life was going next. I decided a new expedition was the best medicine.

Many years ago, I visited New Zealand as a backpacker on the regular tourist trail. This time, I decided I wanted to do it differently. I planned to cycle from Cape Reinga in the north all the way to Bluff on the furthest tip of South Island, stopping off temporarily in Christchurch to race the Speight's Coast to Coast Multisport race from west to east and in Wellington to race the Karopoti National Mountain Biking Championships.

I placed an advert in my local newspaper seeking women interested in forming an adventure racing team. I, of course, was not the first to use newspaper adverts to seek adventure companions. Shackleton is said to have placed an advert for the Imperial Trans-Antarctic Expedition (1914-1917) that read: "Men wanted for hazardous journey. Small wages, bitter cold, long months of complete darkness, constant danger, safe return doubtful. Honour and recognition in event of success."

Although possibly romantically embellished over time, Shackleton's advert reportedly drew thousands of responses, including three from women (who were swiftly rejected). My search for companionship on my adventure yielded just a single response.

That response came from Tori James, a Welsh woman who had summited Everest in 2007. Even though my original shout-out intended to find women to form an adventure racing team, we eventually decided to embark on a cycle tour of New Zealand instead. As we journeyed from the North to the South Island, Tori and I, who set off as strangers, soon grew to become close friends.

Our journey started from the lighthouse at Cape Reinga, the north-westernmost tip of the Aupouri Peninsula. For me, this journey was about reaching the most southerly point of New Zealand, clearing my mind, and finding a path to a new beginning. Enjoying this experience with a new friend was perfect.

During those weeks of constant pedal turning, I had plenty of time to consider my life and career. The scenery of New Zealand became my inspiration, and as I greedily ate up the miles, I became enveloped in my new plans. I was madly in love with adventure racing, and my dream was to turn it into a business of my own. While new pressures would present themselves, one huge pressure was relieved. I would no longer feel guilty allocating time to training, as I had done whilst working in the corporate world. It would be an essential element to my success in my own business. I became so excited about my planning that Tori and I cycled separately on many occasions, meeting up later so I could dwell on my thoughts and structure my future undisturbed.

In New Zealand, sport is a way of life for young and old. Anything and everything seem possible. At one stage on our journey, we hired some kayaks to paddle down the Wanganui River with no form filling or indemnity. In the UK, it often seems we are entangled in red tape and a culture increasingly fixated on safeguarding against potential lawsuits. I found that this burden often discouraged people from trying out something new. In New Zealand, everyone seems willing to experiment with adventure, and sport is as common as having breakfast. I wondered if sport could become a way of life for young and old to enjoy back home in Wales, as it was in New Zealand.

The landscape of North Island was spectacular, with testing mountain passes, expansive open farmland, crystal blue water and an abundance of fleeting friendships. Our overnight camping plans were punctuated by surprise, welcoming offers of a bed for the night. The hospitality was fantastic; we would have made slow progress if we had accepted all the offers.

Our only taste of danger came when we cycled across to the East Coast and were forced to join the dreaded SH1 highway. Life flashed dangerously before my eyes as the noisy, double-loaded logging trucks zipped past at great speed, sucking my bike towards the gap between the first and the second load with frightening regularity. Those split seconds of panic resonated in my mind with a conviction that I was doing absolutely the right thing. Being within inches of my life on that road was a wake-up call that drummed into me the importance of moving on and making my life-long ambition a reality.

I loved the excitement of the unknown and not knowing what lay around the next corner. We met a Maori family in Victoria Valley who kindly gave us a watermelon and introduced us to their pet pig, Molly, who scuttled around, snout to the ground, in search of grubs! We marvelled at New Zealand's largest tree, under which a large group of Cambodian monks were filming each other. The Kauri tree was 2000 years old, 50 metres tall and had a girth of 16 metres.

Stumbling across a veteran's tennis tournament was not in our plan, but we soon found our names on the tournament board, ready to face our first opponents. I was pleased to find that our role was to make up the numbers instead of fulfilling the age criteria. After an afternoon of tennis and a 6-3 match win, we cycled away with our panniers full of freshly made muffins kindly donated by the club secretary to help us on our journey.

Then, we met Nita, a hearty, chatty lady with a round, smiling face waving her family goodbye after a busy weekend of entertaining. When I asked if there was a nearby camping place she responded: "Oh girls, I can't let you camp, you must come inside! I'd be delighted to have your company this evening." Nita farmed beef cattle on 120 acres and recounted tales of her life non-stop, all evening. She also gave us free run of her fridge and said we were doing her a favour by eating everything in it! We obliged with delight.

On my hit list of places to visit was RJ's liquorice factory, not only because it was my favourite snack but because it had proved to be excellent expedition food to add excitement to the bland, dehydrated food diet that adventurers tend to live on to reduce carrying weight. As we approached, my saliva started to flow. I imagined tucking into endless amounts of liquorice, savouring every mouthful, but as we rolled up to the entrance, I nearly fell off my bike with the realisation that it was a bloody Bank Holiday and they were closed! After peering through the window and leaving only drool behind from the array of liquorice on display, I pedalled off disheartened.

Among the many delights of the South Island were beautiful yet pungent baby seals basking in the sunshine next to the azure blue sea along the East Coast. They were cuddly and adorable to look at, but they smelt so strong that we had to take a dip to wash away the acrid smell that lingered in our hair and clothes. In Kaikoura, we found ourselves part of a stag party, complete with chauffeur in the shape of a local policeman who ferried us from our campsite at Goose Bay to the festivities in the pub and back, completely free of charge. He seemed delighted to help us out, perhaps reflecting the lack of crime in the area.

The world-renowned Speights Coast to Coast race is on the hit list for most adventure racers, and fortunately, I was able to fit it into my schedule with the help of the New Zealand Tourist Board, which was kind enough to pay for my entry. The 243-kilometre course from Kumara Beach on the west coast of South Island on the Tasman Sea to Sumner Beach on the Pacific Ocean began in driving wind and rain. The weather was so bad that the 67-kilometre kayaking section on the grade three Waimakariri River, renowned for its deathly rapids, was transferred to the flatter Avon River.

I was disappointed. Just before the change in weather, I had trained on the Waimakariri, and the dangers excited me. But there were plenty more ahead. The run section up Goats Pass involved leaping from boulder to boulder as the water from the mountains gushed across my path. Wow! It was so exhilarating.

After our north-to-south journey, I gazed out over the stormy, ominous ocean as I stood at Bluff, the most southerly point of New Zealand's South Island. I contemplated the icy landmass that lay over 3,000 miles away across the water: Antarctica.

I wondered whether I could continue cycling until I reached the South Pole. At this point, cycling was the only way I wanted to travel, and I felt my journey was by no means at an end. In fact, it felt as if it were only beginning. Like I'd only just opened the door to my future, and I was eager to find what lay ahead. With my renewed enthusiasm, I took a brief moment to change into a Welsh flag for a photo session at Bluff for the Welsh media. Immediately afterwards, I went to the nearest internet café to research the feasibility of cycling in Antarctica.

The only reference that appeared when I searched the words 'cycle Antarctica' on the computer was related to the annual weather cycles on the continent. After more thorough searching, I was surprised to stumble upon a photograph taken in 1911 inside Captain Scott's hut at Cape Evans from his Terra Nova expedition. Due to the dry Antarctic climate, the hut is a time capsule of perfectly preserved artefacts, including provisions, clothing, books and even a mummified sledge dog still in its harness. This particular photograph showed a slick-tyred vintage bicycle that wouldn't have looked out of place on the set of Miss Marple. This was surely Antarctica's first bicycle and was used by the geologist Thomas Griffith Taylor. Taylor rode this bike to the Erebus Glacier tongue as part of a survey expedition. It is noted that exhausted from the journey, he returned on foot, carrying the bicycle with him. I was sure I could do better than that!

After some further frantic and disjointed Google searches, fuelled by a mix of eagerness and the ticking clock of my limited hour at the internet café, I was struck by a surge of exhilaration upon discovering that New Zealand serves as one of the primary gateways to the Antarctic continent.

My mind began to whirr with thoughts on how to plan such an expedition and what type of bike would be best suited. I decided to keep my idea secret to avoid jeopardising my chances of being first and to avoid anyone laughing at me for having such a far-fetched idea.

I had previously read Sir Ranulph Fiennes' excellent biography of Captain Scott. I was reassured that after learning of Cook and Peary's apparent conquest of the North Pole, Amundsen had secretly maintained his revised goal of reaching the South Pole. I preferred to keep my intentions under wraps until I had concrete plans ready and recognised in myself a drive akin to Amundsen's: the aspiration to lead the way, to be the pioneer.

History has shown that skiing is the primary means of travel in Antarctica, and while I take pleasure in various forms of the sport, the South Pole had already been reached by others on skis. I wanted to do things differently and harness my love of cycling, which had been nurtured by my time in New Zealand. Moreover, I was in the best physical shape of my life. Perhaps a cycling expedition to the South Pole could offer an exhilarating adventure and prove a more effective means of travel. The most captivating aspect was that it had never been successfully achieved.

Coinciding with St David's Day, we'd managed to set up a meeting with New Zealand's Prime Minister, John Key. The meeting was arranged through a friend of Tori's, an airline pilot for Air New Zealand, who had flown the Prime Minister to various venues. He was interested in talking to us about our journey because they had plans for building a north-to-south off-road cycle route along the entire length of the country.

I thought it would be wise to take the Prime Minister something typically Welsh, so I presented him with Welsh cakes I'd spent the previous day perfecting. I was surprised to see him tuck straight into them without a confidante testing them first. After a little polite choking, he nodded his head in approval. He was an amenable man, and I felt at ease sitting next to him on the sofa in the executive wing of Parliament Buildings in Wellington in my well-worn, rather smelly lycra. Before leaving Wellington, I participated in The Karapoti National Mountain Bike Championships. I'd just completed a 2400-kilometre journey, so an extra 50 kilometres of tough off-road riding seemed like the icing on the cake.

With over a thousand entrants, the start times were staggered, and it began in Le Monde style as I splashed my way through a thigh-deep river, carrying my bike on my shoulder. I was doing rather well until I was caught behind two competitors cycling at a slower speed. An opportunity came when I decided to pass them on an uphill section, as I knew they would slow down. As we began the climb, one cycled on the left and the other on the right, and a gap opened between them. "I'm coming through," I shouted, but, at that moment, the track narrowed and before I knew it, we were all lying in a heap on the ground. It was totally my fault. "Are you okay," I questioned awkwardly. "Yes, we're fine," one responded, and they cycled off almost immediately. I, on the other hand, took a nasty gash to my arm and leg, and blood splattered down my legs. I pushed my bike to the top of the hill, assessed the damage, took some deep breaths, and steamed ahead. My pace dropped for a while as I tried to build my confidence again. I was now cycling with a throbbing elbow that was swelling like a tennis ball.

The remaining downhills were fast and furious, and I hung on for dear life as I negotiated the technical sections. Flying towards the finish, loving every minute of it, I negotiated the river crossing again, but this time, I misplaced my foot and completely submerged myself and my bike. We both needed a damn good clean anyway! I crossed the finish line in 4hrs 12mins and earned the position of tenth female in the race.

After spending the UK winter months in New Zealand, where the climate was warm and summer-like, it felt strange to think that summer was soon to begin back home. I had left home in confusion about my future, but my experience in New Zealand had fuelled a new beginning. I couldn't wait to put my plans into action. A whole new world of Antarctica awaited, and I couldn't wait to explore it.

# 4. The Most Inhospitable Place on the Planet

"When everything was against me, I focused on the end goal"

I registered my new adventure company, Multisport Ltd, within a month of returning from New Zealand. It wasn't an easy start, and I ended up negotiating my way through many negative responses and searching for legal advice. My persistence paid off, and I received good support from several governing bodies and a grant, which meant I could set up and buy most of the kit I needed to run and organise some of my own adventure races locally.

It was the weekend of my 31st Birthday, and my best friend Claire was over for a visit from Australia. I had planned a night out in Cardiff with some girlfriends, and after returning home at well past 3 am, Claire was unable to stop me from making what could have been a dreadful mistake. I knew Wayne was in America on business, and as we had been in regular contact on Skype, I didn't think twice about calling him. Fuelled by whisky and ginger ale, I blatantly flirted with him. Wayne flew home just a few days later, and we soon became a couple.

To support my new business, I trained as a mountain bike, kayak and CrossFit instructor and qualified as a personal trainer. I read about sports nutrition and incorporated what I learnt from experience. I was soon running multi-sport training courses, and by October 2010, the Burn Series was launched. My first-ever event was Cardiff Burn, with over 200 competitors, some of whom were previous adventure racing world champions. It was a successful start and gave me a real buzz to see others enjoying the sport I loved.

23

I constantly thought about how I would organise my ground-breaking expedition to Antarctica. Historical figures were polar explorers because they were strong-minded men. I was just an ordinary woman with a dream—a dream that I was determined would become a reality.

Over the years, I have learnt how to break down my doubts and sensibly deal with them. I viewed obstacles as hiccups, and their severity made me more determined. I didn't allow my goal to fade, and I was determined to learn everything I could about Antarctica, winter biking and expedition planning. I hoped this approach would open a few more doors and help me achieve my goal. I had no structured plan for the time being, but whenever information became available, I quickly analysed it and stored it away for future use.

I became more involved in the fat biking community and followed blogs from people, mainly in the USA or Canada, who seemed to be serious winter bikers. I needed to learn more about this mesmerising sport. Fat bikes provided improved grip and traction on soft or snowy terrain, but they seemed clumsier to ride and were much heavier than a standard mountain bike. I had a lot to learn before I could be sure of the best cycle for Antarctica.

I continued to study Antarctica in depth. I learnt about its history, studied expedition blogs and became familiar with weather patterns and conditions that I would likely encounter on the big white continent. I poured over the National Maritime Museum's compendium of facts about Antarctica. Each entry fired off a rocket of desire inside me. One page read:

'Antarctica is the most inhospitable place on the planet. The lowest recorded temperature is minus 89.2 degrees Celsius. Once on the Polar Plateau, the ice cap is up to four kilometres thick, and explorers are likely to suffer from altitude sickness as much as frostbite.'

Antarctica is the fifth-largest continent, covering around 14 million square kilometres. It's bigger than Europe and double the size of Australia. Most of Antarctica has no life, but there are birds, including penguins, sea creatures such as seals, whales, and fish, and a few simple yet hardy mosses and lichens near the coastal fringes.

Antarctica has been blanketed in ice for approximately 34 million years. This started when the Earth's climate experienced a significant cooling, leading to the formation of the ice sheet. Around the same time, the continent gradually drifted to its current location over the South Pole.

Palaeontologists have discovered fossils, including dinosaurs, in the rocks of the Antarctic Peninsula and the Transantarctic Mountains. These findings support the theory that Antarctica was once part of the larger landmass known as Gondwana, which is consistent with the concepts of continental drift and plate tectonics. During the Mesozoic era, from 252 to 66 million years ago, the area that is now an icy wilderness was once covered with dense, temperate forests and was home to dinosaurs.

Surprisingly, Antarctica is described as a desert, with, on average, just 20 cm of snow falling each year at the South Pole, making it the driest place on Earth. Consequently, Antarctic blizzards really consist of ice crystals being whipped up by the wind that is sometimes so fine that they can lodge between the slits of your closed eyes.

Over 90% of the world's fresh water is locked up in Antarctica's ice sheet. Over half the Southern Ocean freezes in winter, doubling Antarctica's size. Only recently has the use of aircraft given Antarctic explorers an alternative means of supply.

The story of the South Pole's conquest harks back to 1909 when it stood among the remaining grand geographic prizes. While America's foremost polar explorers, Cook and Peary, were preoccupied with being first to the North Pole, the Admiralty and Royal Geographical Society chose Captain Robert Falcon Scott to lead the British expedition to Antarctica.

Scott left his position in the Royal Navy, where he was developing expertise on the new type of torpedo warfare. His approach was methodical, and he dedicated three years to scientific inquiry and meticulous planning for the polar journey. Roald Amundsen and his Norwegian team surprised Scott by upending his strategy. Learning of Cook and Peary's apparent conquest of the North Pole, Amundsen stealthily rerouted his ship, the Fram, toward the Antarctic.

Scott, known for his appreciation of the arts and sciences and his expressive diary entries, stood in contrast to the stoic and result-driven Amundsen, who regarded adventure as merely the by-product of inadequate planning. Scott's team was sizeable for the era, comprising 65 individuals, including Terra Nova's crew, 12 scientists, and one photographer. Of these, five embarked for the Pole. The inclusion of a fifth member was a last-minute decision.

Conversely, Amundsen's contingent, akin to modern ultra-marathoners, consisted of nine robust men proficient in skiing, navigation, and dog handling. Five elite members, including champion skier Olav Bjaaland, led the race to the Pole.

Amundsen had become adept in survival techniques through his time with the nomadic Netsilik people in Canada. His transport methods were streamlined: Greenland Huskies hauling 400-kilogram sledges, which, as they neared their goal, were systematically sacrificed to feed the team, thus lightening the load. Of the 50 dogs that set out, only 11 returned to base camp.

Scott's more complex logistics involved motor sledges, Manchurian ponies, and a few Siberian Huskies, with the crew eventually shouldering the burden through man-hauling. Predictably, the motor sledges malfunctioned, the ponies succumbed to the cold, and the Huskies were too few. The men's gruelling trek, dragging their supplies, led to extended travel times, malnutrition and starvation. Scott's expedition relied on standard, hard, and less energy-dense British army biscuits, while Amundsen's team used specially formulated, nutrient-rich pemmican biscuits better suited for the extreme Antarctic conditions. The Norwegians were even able to discard surplus provisions to ease their burden.

Amundsen's team departed the Ross Ice Shelf on October 19, 1911. They spanned the 1,380-kilometre distance to the Pole in 56 days, setting up a tent at their goal on December 14, 1911. They left a letter to King Haakon VII of Norway and a courteous request for Scott to deliver it should they not return. They returned to their base, Framheim, in 43 days.

Just under a month later, on November 1, 1911, Scott's party set off from Cape Evans. Seventy-nine days after, on January 17th, 1912, after an arduous 1,500-kilometre journey, they arrived at the Pole to discover that Amundsen had beaten them to it.

Scott's disappointment was palpable in these extracts from his diary on that day: "The Pole. Yes, but under very different circumstances from those expected. We have had a horrible day—add to our disappointment a headwind 4 to 5, with a temperature -22°, and companions labouring on with cold feet and hands. ...The Norwegians have forestalled us and are first at the Pole. It is a terrible disappointment, and I am very sorry for my loyal companions. All the day dreams must go; it will be a wearisome return."

Indeed, Scott's team suffered terribly on their return trek in awful weather, far worse than Amundsen encountered. During that season, temperatures reportedly plunged to around minus 50 degrees Celsius, creating an impossible survival scenario for the exhausted and malnourished men.

The final tragedy of Scott and his comrades, just eleven miles from One Ton Depot (which would have offered a chance of potential rescue and relief), was not discovered until around eight months after they died. Even in the face of grim conditions during their return trip, as evidenced by letters and diary entries discovered alongside their bodies, Scott and his team continued transporting geological samples they had gathered from the mountains near the Beardmore Glacier. This fact serves as a poignant testament to their dedication to the scientific objectives of their mission and their goal of reaching the Pole.

Roald Amundsen's attainment of the South Pole stands as a masterclass in expedition planning and execution, a stark contrast to the saga of endurance and sacrifice recorded in Scott's eloquent writings. Amundsen's calculated approach underscored his deep understanding of polar survival, and his team's victory was a product of adaptability and meticulous preparation that emphasised efficiency and the well-being of his crew without any loss of life.

I was entranced to learn about this incredible new world's physical, historical and geographical nature. It was no wonder that a fantastic amount of research in all fields was going on in its pristine environment. Close to 50 countries had signed up to the Antarctic Treaty System set up in 1961 to ensure that the planet's only continent without a native human population would remain a reserve for scientists alone. The treaty forbids military activity and is a diplomatic expression of the operational and scientific cooperation that can be achieved on the ice. To me, that meant it was the most peaceful place on Earth.

For cosmologists and physicists, the sky above the South Pole, bereft of pollution or light from radio waves, provided the cleanest environment on Earth to site amazingly powerful telescopes that tell us about the history of our world and the universe beyond. Palaeobotanists found remarkably well-preserved plant fossils in the rocks beneath the ice sheet, and in 2017, the fossilised remains of a 71-million-year-old forest were discovered near the Transantarctic Mountain Range.

The scientific community has been closely monitoring the sobering effects of melting ice caps and the consequent rise in the world's ocean levels. The Pine Island Glacier in Antarctica is a prime example, being one of the fastest-melting glaciers on the continent and a significant contributor to sea-level rise. Recent studies have revealed that the glacier loses billions of tons of ice yearly. This rapid ice loss is mainly due to warm ocean waters eroding the glacier from underneath, a process thoroughly investigated by scientists involved in Britain's iStar programme. The imbalance caused by more ice melting at the base than the accumulation at the top is a concerning trend. While it is difficult to predict the exact impact, the full melting of the West Antarctic Ice Sheet, including the Pine Island Glacier, could raise global sea levels by several meters over the coming centuries.

As I researched, odd facts popped up about life in Antarctica today that were equally fascinating. Surprisingly, there were almost 2,500 applicants for a postmaster role that also included the job of counting penguins! It was home to seven churches, one a Catholic ice cave and another built entirely of shipping containers. Perhaps the comfort of religion was an important sanctuary in a place where nature ruled so harshly.

I learnt that the most common entry and exit point for expeditions into Antarctica was through a company called Antarctic Logistics & Expeditions (ALE) that operates a base camp at Union Glacier, which lies in the middle of the Heritage Range in the Ellsworth Mountains. ALE chose this location because of its relatively calm summer months. The exposed blue ice, further down the glacier, was perfect for creating a blue ice runway for the inbound and outbound Ilyushin 76 TD aircraft used to transport passengers and equipment to and from Antarctica and Punta Arenas in Chile. I learnt that entry from New Zealand was mainly the preserve of scientists who worked at the American-owned McMurdo Station near Captain Scott's hut on Ross Island.

Few expeditions began from Union Glacier, but logistics were in place for transporting expedition members to common start points such as Hercules Inlet, a twenty-minute flight from Union Glacier. This was where most people attempting a traverse from the continent's edge began their long and arduous journey to the South Pole.

Hercules Inlet is a large, narrow, ice-filled inlet that forms part of the southwestern margin of the Ronne Ice shelf. The route from there covers approximately one thousand kilometres and historically takes between 24 and 81 days to complete by skis. The longest-standing human-powered record on this route stood at 24 days and was held by Norwegian skier Christian Eide. Apart from the beginning of this route, where there are some known crevasse fields, it is in the main a straight line south. However, from all accounts, it was tough going.

I researched blogs by adventurers who described challenges such as soft, deep snow and sastrugi—steep, wave-like ridges of snow sculpted by the wind, resembling frozen sea waves. These formations, parallel to the wind direction, can reach a metre in height and are particularly difficult to navigate on a bike.

All the blogs I was reading were from skiers, so their opinions on passable or impassable terrain would be very different to my view of going on a bike. I was still inexperienced in winter biking, so needed to test for myself whether it was possible to cycle through soft snow and the dreaded sastrugi.

Fortunately, the winter of 2010 provided the perfect opportunity when the UK endured minus ten-degree temperatures and snow that lay for over three weeks. My parents' home turned out to be the perfect place to test my ideas. We lived on a tranquil, eighty-acre deer park in the Vale of Glamorgan.

Enclosed by ancient stone walls, the landscape has remained pristine and virtually unchanged for over 350 years. As the first snowfall lay glistening in the winter sun, I was out on my mountain bike as early as possible.

The trees were adorned in a lavish coat of snow, each limb meticulously highlighted with a heavy layer that resembled sprinklings of fine icing sugar. This turned the landscape into a mesmerising winter wonderland, and the deep, soft carpet of snow persisted steadfastly, day after day.

The Park, with its many hills and valleys, was the perfect place to test my ability to ride my mountain bike in the snow. As the snowfall persisted and the temperatures plunged even lower, the conditions only improved, with the snow crisping under the frigid minus 10 degrees Celsius chill. This presented the perfect chance for me to test my endurance against the prolonged cold, resisting the urge to pedal through the Park to the beckoning warmth of the house, where the log-burning stove was on daily duty.

After several attempts, I realised that cycling up anything remotely steep in the snow was nearly impossible. Heading downhill repeatedly ended with a painful knock to my head, knees and elbows as the bike skidded from underneath me. On the few flat sections, such as the upper and lower valleys of the Park, my puff just ran out as I tried to cycle through the deep snow. I refused to give up.

For almost ten days, I tried different techniques, such as tyre pressure and adjusting my weight distribution on the bike. I would also need to carry the equivalent of my body weight in equipment. Where was I going to put that? Carrying it on the bike would be impossible, so I considered a sledge an option. I rigged up a homemade sledge as a trial. It was even more of a disaster. Perhaps rideability could be improved using a fat bike with wider tyres. It was the only light at the end of the tunnel.

As the snow began to melt, I felt disheartened. I had yet to make any headway in learning to cycle in deep, soft snow. All I'd gained were some bruises, very cold feet and, for some reason, an insatiable desire to persist with my idea. The fact that no one had ever cycled to the South Pole before was always on my mind.

Visualising myself standing at the Pole, having just achieved this dream, was an image too overpowering to abandon. I was driven by the desire to be first, and my failure to date did not convince me that it couldn't be done. I would just need to think differently about the whole thing. Something deep inside me refused to be beaten.

In 2011, I identified a huge gap in the adventure sports market and began to target my adventure races towards families. These races were more local and simpler, lasting half a day but ultimately following the same format as the adventure races in which I had taken part. The idea was to attract both parents and children to experience the fun of adventure together in a beautiful setting. I had found a niche market.

2011 was also a very successful year of racing for me. I was now competing locally in running, cycling, and triathlons, and I continued with the occasional expedition race further afield. I raced solo for most of the year and clocked up some of my best results. Following the Wainwright route, I competed in the Adidas Terrex Coast-to-Coast race across England. I'd previously run this race in 2009 as a solo and come second. This time, I'd decided to race it in a team. I joined up with two brothers who were experienced fell runners, and together with my kayaking and biking expertise, we were a good combination. After four days of racing across the country on foot, bike, and kayak, we ran to victory to claim the title.

My winning streak continued, and I won the Scotland Coast to Coast race in September 2011. It was a run, bike and kayak event from the North Sea coast near Inverness over 105 miles of rocky going via Loch Ness, Glencoe, Fort William and Ben Nevis, which started in the dark and finished in the dark, crossing Scotland in one day. I was cold and wet, but I was the first female to complete the run section, which put me in good spirits. It was one of the first races where Wayne was my support, ensuring I had all the right kit at each transition. He soon realised my desire to win. The mountain biking was single trails through forests, climbing massive hills with the most spectacular scenery all around me. Racing for 13 hours alone was a tough affair, followed by four hours of sitting in my kayak. As I paddled the length of Loch Ness looking out for the monster, I felt so stiff and tired that I wasn't sure if I'd be able to walk again.

# 5. A Life-Threatening Training Race on the Central Siberian Plateau

"Push yourself hard, but stop before finding your limit"

I have always enjoyed the biting cold. It makes me feel alive and spurs me to use my body even more. If I had an option to be too hot or cold, I would choose cold any day. I believed that by physically pushing my body, I would create the heat needed to keep me alive. The challenge of survival in temperatures that the body was not designed to cope with excited me. However, I knew I needed to train in these conditions before attempting my ultimate challenge of cycling to the South Pole, where conditions would be even harsher.

It was time to test myself as a solo adventurer. I needed something that could really scare me, and during an internet search, I came up with the perfect solution—the Siberian Black Ice race. I had one major problem. How on earth was I going to explain this one to Wayne?

Until now, he'd been most accommodating with my crazy ideas and extreme view on life, and I felt his patience might be waning. I suspected he wanted a stable, grounded, loving and caring girlfriend, not one who was constantly dreaming up crazy, dangerous plans, especially as every adventure just fuelled my desire for more.

Our relationship was by no means perfect. We both had strong personalities, which led to some fierce clashes, though every clash seemed to bring us that little bit closer. Sometimes, I think we just needed a good argument to have the excuse to make up again. Both of us were highly driven and stubborn, and we wanted to be right. We had taken different paths in life, but fundamentally, our values and principles were the same, which seemed to be our saviour. Now I had decided on my next challenge, I had to work out a way of breaking the news to Wayne.

Wayne was setting up a new office in the Lake District and flying down to Cardiff most weekends so we could be together. I sat nervously in the car under the bridge, which we'd chosen as our meeting point, to avoid the parking fee at the airport. I practised what I would say in the car mirror. "I've decided I'm going to take part in the Black Ice Race, which will involve cycling the length of Lake Baikal in Siberia, which is the deepest freshwater lake in the world." After a few rehearsals, I decided that whatever came naturally would be best as it would probably sound frightful to him whatever I said.

As he walked over to my car, I felt the familiar surge of excitement in my stomach. "Gosh, I've missed you," I said, flinging my arms around his shoulders.

"Good to be here. It's been a long week," he responded. We jumped into the driver and passenger seats, desperate to begin our weekend together.

Before even leaving the vicinity of the airport, I felt the words coming out of my mouth. "I've found the perfect training race for me to do in preparation for the South Pole. I'm going to cycle across Lake Baikal on the central Siberian plateau, but don't worry, it will be frozen," I spluttered. Wayne's smile lost its glimmer. Silence fell in the car, and I realised immediately how stupid I must have sounded. "What I mean is that it's a controlled race under controlled conditions," I continued. Oh damn! Now, I was lying. I was both stupid and a liar.

"Okay," said Wayne with irritation in his voice. "Let's talk about it later; right now, I need to relax and enjoy the weekend." Deep down, he knew I had made up my mind, and deep down, I knew I would have to work twice as hard to make it all okay. I felt a streak of guilt that I had already put a damper on his weekend. I knew he was very keen for me to come and live with him in the Lake District, so half selfishly and half selflessly, I followed up by saying: "I've been thinking, why don't I move up to the Lakes with you, I can, after all, run my business from there in the winter".

It was October 2011 and the Black Ice Race was in March 2012. With its much higher chance of snow, the Lake District would be a brilliant area for my training. Before long, we found ourselves living in Bowness-on-Windermere, renting a three-bedroom apartment on the edge of Lake Windermere. The location was stunning. The weather, however, was atrocious. It rained incessantly all day and night, every day and night. I spent some days with Wayne in his office, helping his management team with their strategy and business improvement. The rest of the time, I was out on my mountain bike.

One day, my cycle training didn't go as planned. "I'm lost, Wayne!" I admitted meekly down the office phone line. It was 2.45 pm on November 21. I'd been on my bike all day with no map or supplies, pretending I could get away with it. I'd been on roads, tracks and mountains and now had no clue where I was. "I'm in a Board meeting," he replied impatiently. "I'll pass you over to Robert."

Robert was the Operations Director of INOV8 at the time. "Oh no, what is everyone in the boardroom going to think of me now!" I said to myself, squirming with embarrassment.

Luckily, Robert was local to the area and knew it inside out. He could give me directions after I explained what I could see and where I had been. This involved following the verge of a busy dual carriageway for about four miles before I returned to the country lanes that I recognised. At last, I was able to find my way home.

I cycled every day, and as the light faded by 4 pm, I took to cycling on my turbo trainer on our balcony in the dark. The snow began to fall in December, and my training became more realistic. On one outing with a new cycling friend, I took a nasty fall off my bike on a very icy single track and slit my chin open. I spent the rest of the afternoon in the hospital, having to be glued back together again. I decided not to call Wayne until I was back on my feet because it would likely be the last straw.

The Siberian Black Ice race aimed to journey by unmotorised means unsupported from one end of Lake Baikal to the other—a total of 636 kilometres. Running, skiing, skating, or cycling were the options. I chose cycling. It was the first time I'd attempted anything on this scale as a solo competitor, so I had some intricate planning to complete and a steep learning curve to travel.

We had industrial-sized freezers at home in the deer park where venison was stored. Fortunately for me, after a bumper year of sales, one of them was now empty—perfect for testing my equipment in freezing conditions. Scurrying around our park yard, I located five large plastic containers, which I filled with water and placed in the freezer to make large blocks of ice. I pulled out a measuring tape to check the dimensions of the freezer and then worked out that if I broke down my titanium mountain bike into parts, I could fit the whole lot into the freezer alongside the plastic containers. Even though I had reassurance from the manufacturers, I wanted to test whether the titanium on my bike would survive a few nights at minus 19 degrees Celsius.

I also needed to test my cooking equipment. I decided to invest in an Arctic expedition stove that was advertised as a world leader in the field of extreme condition exploration. Upon its arrival, I excitedly ripped open the MSR Arctic cooker box and pulled out numerous parts. As usual, I didn't read the instructions, but fortunately, it all seemed to fit together in what appeared to be the correct order. I had also ordered three empty MSR fuel bottles, one of which I filled with petrol from the 100-gallon tank that stood on stilts in the yard.

I aimed to mimic conditions on Lake Baikal and make a delicious cup of coffee from melting the ice blocks I had put in the freezer earlier, using only my ice pick, some petrol, one match, and my brand new MSR cooker. My treasured ice pick, made by my father with a pickaxe on one end and a hammer on the other, was inscribed with the message: 'Siberian Black Ice Race—Keep going!'

In hasty anticipation, I struck the match, and it blew out immediately. This confirmed that a mishap like this on the ice of Lake Baikal could be fatal, so I had to take a variety of fire-lighting equipment with me, including lighters, matches, and flint fire steel, which works by creating a spark.

Breaking down ice blocks with my ice axe took longer than I expected. I timed exactly how long each size would take to thaw and then to boil, using a variety of temperatures on my stove until I was satisfied with a formula. The one variable I couldn't recreate was the outside temperature. I decided against the option of locking myself and a bottle of burning petrol into my parent's freezer, and I left that variable to chance.

I also needed to research a suitable sleeping bag. Clever marketing makes them sound better than they are. A sleeping bag rated at minus 35 degrees Celsius doesn't mean you'll be comfortable at minus 35 degrees Celsius; it simply means that provided you wear the required layers of clothing, you are less likely to die of hypothermia. There were also male and female temperature ratings, assuming men could sustain colder temperatures. Fortunately, I didn't need to research further as an ultra-runner friend, who had competed in the Yukon Arctic Ultra race the previous year, agreed to lend me her sleeping bag, with the bonus that it was rated to withstand minus 50 degrees Celsius.

Equally crucial for my survival on the ice was a suitable tent that would balance low weight, great strength and a degree of comfort.

After plenty of consultation with people in the know and reading between the lines of the online marketing jargon, I chose a one-person Hilleberg tent that I could assemble quickly without instructions. As I crept inside, I realised how small it was. Less room would encourage me to cycle more and sleep less.

Lake Baikal lies in the central Siberian plateau, surrounded by mountains and forests, much of which is protected as a national park. The lake has 27 islands, the largest of which is Olkhon, which is 72 kilometres long. 330 rivers feed the lake, which drains through a single river called the Angara. My journey across this massive, ominous lake began at the mouth of the Angara, near the west end of the lake.

I arrived in the ancient Cossack city of Irkutsk in the bitter cold with my mountain bike. Against conventional wisdom, I decided not to use a fat bike. I had studied aerial maps of the lake and realised there was more likely to be exposed ice than deep snow. I had about 50 metal studs in each ice breaker tyre, and I had bought some large flat downhill pedals to accommodate my massive polar boots.

The race was due to start within 24 hours of landing, and with nine hours of jet lag hanging over me, there was little time to acclimatise. After some media frenzy at Irkutsk airport, as this was the first race of its kind to be held in Siberia, we were transported promptly to our hotel. I was overflowing with questions as I chatted incessantly with competitors from all over the world, weighing up the competition and comparing notes on kit, gear and tactics.

My confidence surged and dwindled as we discussed our varying abilities. Most competitors had been on polar training, but I'd never experienced solo survival in extreme temperatures, and I was nervous. I felt comfortable about the distance but worried about the cold and racing for the first time in my life on ice—ice that, according to the organisers, was starting to crack due to unseasonably warm temperatures. Three other competitors had chosen to cycle. Two were using fat bikes, and one local Russian had opted for his mountain bike. I felt confident in my choice of bike but soon realised that I had my work cut out since the Russian was a national cyclocross champion.

The organisers confirmed they would have a hovercraft on the lake ready to deal with emergencies. We signed out the satellite phones we had hired from the organisation, and it seemed we were well covered in case of an emergency. The true picture that was about to unfold was very different.

The afternoon flew by, packed with planning, last-minute shopping, briefings and safety checks before hitting the pillow just before midnight. Only as I lay awake for most of the night, watching the minutes tick by, I had time to contemplate what may lie ahead. As I dipped in and out of sleep, I was scared, frightened, excited and thrilled all at the same time. A jumble of emotions rocked the night. The last time I looked at my watch it was 6.42 am. At 7.45 am, my alarm sounded, and race day had arrived.

To my surprise, some competitors received last-minute lessons on using a GPS on the bus to the race start. Phew! At least I was fully confident with a GPS, so maybe I'm one step ahead already, I thought.

As the bus rolled up into the quaint little town of Listvyanka, I caught my first glance of Lake Baikal. I had studied many maps and photographs of the lake, yet it looked vastly more ominous than the almost familiar picture I had created in my mind. The lake's surface gleamed in its primordial coat of ice, interrupted by massive mounds of snow that sat like dense clouds and obliterated its scale. I stood in amazement. Then, the biting cold took hold and forced me to join the others in the hotel on the lake's edge, where we received our final race briefing before the start.

I tucked into a massive lunch of beetroot and meat soup, large rissoles, boiled potatoes and pickled mushrooms before arriving on the start line at 2.30 pm along with 29 other nervous competitors. A host of Russian journalists interrupted my thoughts, questioning us about the race. I felt anxious during the final check-up, but once the countdown began, I felt confident, happy and ready for action. I am going to race hard. I am going to win this.

Setting off in deep snow was tough, and I was forced to ride and push my bike intermittently. Visibility was low, and when I glanced around at the other competitors, they appeared to melt into the surroundings. Would I ever see them again? I'd kept an eye on the Russian biker who knew the area, and I traced his every move. His progress was impressive, and he seemed to know the best route to take. As conditions improved, the two of us increased our speed and steamed off at the head of the field.

After about two hours, my right pedal fell off to my utter dismay. I'd made a massive error by not tightening it up sufficiently. My hard pedalling had damaged the thread on the inside of the pedal crank. The fear of being unable to continue due to a stupid mistake so early in the race forced me to find a solution. I removed the loose aluminium and tried repeatedly to get the pedal on, but it just wouldn't sit straight. I decided to bind the pedal shaft with some tape, and much to my delight, the repair bit, and I could screw it in.

Twenty minutes had passed, I was freezing cold, and a few others had caught up with me, but at least I was still in the race. By this time, the Russian cyclist I had been following had disappeared into the distance. As I rounded the first headland, I was exposed to the full force of the Lake Baikal wind. It blew ferociously in my face, biting into my cheeks, almost splitting the flesh. There was no glory in the low visibility and incessant wind; it was bleak, cold and empty.

As the conditions worsened, it became more haunting, and the daylight turned to impenetrable greyness. The wind was too strong to ride, so I had to haul my bike and kit alongside me as well as I could. Other competitors were also struggling behind me with their pulks. I took comfort because we were all in it together, fighting the elements.

By 7.30 pm and after five hours on the go, the light began to diminish, and along with a few others, we fought the incessant gale to erect our tents. The lake's surface was a mixture of completely transparent black ice and snow patches, some small, some very large. My race plan had been to try and cycle well into the night to gain a few extra kilometres over my competitors, but for safety reasons, I abandoned my plan on the first night, "Perhaps tomorrow I can cycle through the night," I said to myself.

The wind died down overnight, and the temperature fell to minus 27 degrees Celsius. Thanks to all my kit and clothing, I was warm. My worst worry was the thundering sound of the ice cracking beneath me. I lay rigid inside my sleeping bag, listening constantly to the dull cracking sound, praying the volume would not explode into a cacophony of shattering ice. My ears ached as I continually strained to detect an increase in the reverberations.

I had not prepared myself to deal with the continuous sound of cracking ice. It was deeply unsettling, and I dozed fitfully all night, dreaming uncomfortably as I imagined my legs were engulfed in torrents of icy water, followed by my waist, followed by my chest and finally my neck… The next morning, the snow had been cleared by the wind, and only solitary, fluffy patches remained surrounded by black ice. The lake's surface was covered with millions upon millions of tiny hairline cracks. The purity and clarity of the water, combined with the temperature drop, had produced metre-thick sheets of clear icy glass, over which I had to cycle.

It was a surreal experience to be riding on black ice. Seeing straight through the icy glass surface into a dark abyss below that stretched over a mile deep was petrifying. My brain worked overtime trying to calculate which cracks were dangerous and which cracks could be negotiated. The thickness of the ice seemed to vary drastically, yet I could never tell precisely by how much. I took little comfort from my naivety. The pressure of my wheels spearheaded a fan of fractures all around me, and at times, my wheels sunk suddenly and unexpectedly where an ice layer had weakened. It was terrifying.

I feared the next fracture would envelop me, my bike and my kit as I slowly plunged to the bottom of Lake Baikal. I had to prepare for the worst, so I devised a plan. If I fell through a gap in the ice, I would attempt to spread my body out as wide as I could, hoping to catch an edge of the ice that would allow me to pull myself free. I gazed down at my large boots and wondered whether I could kick them off easily, as that would reduce my weight by two kilograms. Once filled with Lake Baikal water, they would be almost double that weight. I had to get rid of them; otherwise, I would most certainly sink. I also had to ensure that there was no way my clothing would get caught on the bike. What if my bike handle caught in my coat pocket and dragged me under? I felt clumsily around with my gloves to check that my pockets were all done up tightly. I tucked away any dangling cords from my jacket and trousers. Only now did I realise the benefits of skiing or skating as they had poles to help them climb out of the water. If only I had carried some ice picks around my neck.

My focus on pedalling had begun to deteriorate, and I found myself in a 'what if' panic. I had never faced anything like this before and felt unprepared to cope with the worst. I have always been a keen planner, but this time, it was surreal and happening too quickly to gather my thoughts and experience. I'd never felt so scared.

It was a tough ten-hour day. I only allowed myself a five-minute stop every hour to down some energy food and take a quick swig from my flask buried inside my jacket to prevent it from freezing. Progress was slow, and I only managed to cover about 50 kilometres even though I had pedalled 89 kilometres. The walkers were still in sight, like tiny birds in the background, which caused me concern.

I reassessed my original plan to cycle well into the night. I decided that no torch, however powerful, would avert the possibility of the ice opening up as I plunged to my death in the icy waters below. Travelling at any speed in the dark would increase my stopping time, which could lead to disaster. I had to accept that I probably wouldn't catch the Russian up again. Now, survival was my only aim.

On day three, the ice was smooth and undisturbed, and there was a gentle tailwind. It was the day I'd dreamt of, as it could be enough to put me way ahead of the other competitors. The sun was shining, and

I felt motivated. I hit a top speed of 47 kilometres per hour.

Nearing the southern tip of Olkhon Island, I decided to stay close to the coast, as I wanted to get a good view of the gap between the mainland and the island. This proved to be an error of judgment as I soon hit a large field of broken sastrugi ice. We had been warned of open water in this area as two days before the race, a car had gone through the ice, and the truck that went out to rescue it also went through the ice. To my left and right, sharp sections of jagged ice rose menacingly all around me, and I had no choice but to begin the arduous task of partially carrying and pushing my bike. It took me about an hour to see clear ice again, and I'd barely covered two kilometres. Back on the bike, my left knee was beginning to give me some pain, which had started the day before when I'd spent ten hours pedalling hard into a 60-mile-an-hour wind.

The day felt long, and after two falls off my bike onto jagged, broken ice, one of which saw me land very heavily on my helmet, I arrived at the midway checkpoint on the northern part of Olkhon Island. I was the third competitor to arrive. The excellent news diverted my thoughts from my thumping headache and bruises as I was checked over by the medic in the organiser's cabin. "How is the race going?" I asked her. She replied vaguely, without making eye contact. "We have lost some competitors who are now out of the race."

The shock of her words frightened me, but I decided not to inquire further in case it jeopardised my mental strength. I was given my transition bag, containing all the provisions I had packed to get me through the second part of the race. I delved inside apprehensively to check I had sufficient supplies. I pulled out some freeze-dried packets of expedition food and another five litres of fuel, which we were recommended to carry. As I had only used half a litre over the last three days, I decided to leave it as I could do without the extra weight, thanks to my precision ice melting practice back home.

I knew how much fuel I needed to prepare my freeze-dried meals for up to a week, and I also had a plan B for acquiring fresh water if I ran out of fuel. I could use my ice screws where the ice was thin to hollow out water for drinking, and with the help of the tube from my hydration system, I could suck up the water. As I placed my allocated fuel back in the pile, I was stung with the sobering thought that this would not be an option in Antarctica. There would be no available water, and bad weather conditions could convert a three-week expedition into a two-month expedition. Not carrying ample amounts of fuel in Antarctica would be stupid, irresponsible and outright naive.

However, I decided to live on the edge right now, which was necessary to test myself if a difficult situation arose.

That evening, I was pleased to be reunited with the other two cyclists still in the race. We settled in for the evening in the comfort of our tents and shared some wine and cheese, which the boys had tucked away in their transition bag, to complement their freeze-dried food. The boys appeared to be the perfect team. Jez was a well-spoken, organised type, but he needed his mate, tousle-haired Matt, to provide the steerage and experience. As an ex-Royal Marine, Matt was fit and inventive and the kind of man who would gobble up any challenge. "Take a swig of this, Maria; it will put hairs on your chest," said Matt as he passed me the wine bottle. I slurped down a mouthful and coughed at the bitter-sweet flavour. My palate had become accustomed to freeze-dried food, and I could not cope with this sudden liquid deviation. I gave up on the cheese, and just a nibble seemed to sit uncomfortably in my throat. Nevertheless, I enjoyed the boys' banter.

"I can't believe that nine competitors have already been pulled off the race," said Jez, who, unlike me, had questioned the medic earnestly. A couple of them had frostbite, and others carried more kit than they could manage. Can you believe it? Some idiot even managed to burn down his tent."

"They were the two Royal Engineers who assumed they knew much more than the rest of us when we were chatting on the start line," said Matt.

"Oh! And have you heard they have even lost track of one competitor altogether," said Jez.

"They haven't heard from him in 24 hours," Matt added.

"Surely, the emergency team will find him," I said faintly.

I felt shocked but silently proud to have come this far. There was something special about being totally immersed in something that scared me yet made me feel totally in control of my life. Like all adventurers, I was pushing to near my limit. My instinct was my guardian angel, and I felt something deep inside would stop me before I went too far. At the same time, I never wanted to look back and feel I could have done more.

As usual, I was up early the following day, packing away my tent and kit. I gave the lads, still motionless in their tent, a shout. They took their time to pack up, but I decided to stick with them as the organisers had warned us, yet again, that ice conditions were not good at the top of the island and we must report any large areas of broken ice.

"I am nervous but determined to finish the race," I told myself. My original race plan had been reconfigured, and I was more at ease to go with the flow.

Soon after we set off, we came across a large 200-metre crack in the ice over which we had to find a safe passage. Luckily, Matt volunteered to go first to test the ice and Jez and I were more than happy to let him do so. Each time we found an area that looked stable enough, Matt would go first, and we'd then push his bike across to him. I would go next with my bike, followed by Jez and his bike.

We continued this routine for about two hours when we heard a thunderous roar about 20 metres behind me and only three metres behind Matt. Another massive crack had appeared. The splintered ice rose angrily, and lake water bubbled to the surface. Matt yelled, and we pedalled hard. Stopping a few minutes later, we viewed the gaping chasm behind us. It was a lucky escape. The constant sound of cracking ice that I had got used to when cycling increased in pitch from a low grumbling to a deafening, high-pitched crashing sound as my wheel rode over the ice. My right knee was beginning to hurt again, and to make matters worse, ahead of us was a massive sastrugi field.

For the next three hours, Matt, Jez and I pulled, tugged, swore and threw our bikes around as we struggled to make progress over the eight-kilometre stretch of ice field, which was seemingly impassable. Fortunately, the ice studs that Wayne had put in my boots helped, and I could balance precariously on ice slabs and jump from one to the next, hauling, pulling and pushing my bike awkwardly alongside me.

It was late in the day when we finally hit flat ice with snowy patches. We approached another extensive, long crack in the ice where we had to test the stability and this time, I decided to check it out first. While balancing on my left leg and probing the ice with my right, the surface suddenly broke, and I plunged into the frigid water and ice up to my thigh. Matt was quick to grab my jacket and pull me out. The water poured into my left boot, soaking my socks and thermals. It was freezing cold, but there was no time for self-pity; the area was unstable, and we had to move on quickly.

As we scanned the ice for a good spot to cross, Matt had the great idea of building an ice ramp that we would cycle at speed towards so that we would clear the opening on our bikes. I used my ice axe to carve out broken ice and pile it leading up to and over the gap. Matt went first and did a spectacular jump. Next, it was my turn, and as I approached, Matt yelled that I needed more speed. As I turned a circle to pick up speed, I lost the exact point of crossing from my vision and approached a metre off target. My front wheel sank into the water. I winded myself badly as I fell from my bike and slid along the ice. I lay there with tears pouring down my face. "What the hell are you doing?" Matt said, laughing at my predicament. Cold and shivering with a bad knee and a bruised ego, I got back on my bike, bit my lip with determination and buried my pain.

# 6. Cracking Ice

*"When doubt sets in, follow your instinct"*

The wind was so ferocious during the night that we tied our tents together for extra security. I nursed my bruises with arnica and stayed awake most of the night, listening to the incessant howling of the wind. The ice I'd been crossing yesterday had been very unstable, and the sound of it cracking haunted me into the night.

I sensed the deep reverberations of the moving ice, and whether it was in my imagination or not, I could feel the cold water, not far below, sucking heat from my body. I catnapped, dreaming yet again that my feet sunk into the icy depths and the lower part of my sleeping bag was sucked into the freezing water. At any moment, I feared I would sink into the abyss.

The following day, the mounds of snow had completely hidden our tents due to the force of the overnight wind. I spent an hour shovelling the snow off my tent in the dark before I could pack it away.

As I set off, the day was dawning, and the wind seemed even stronger. Now, well into the race, my confidence was growing. I had not accounted for the conditions getting worse. Suddenly, a fierce crosswind propelled me at great speed in the wrong direction. Moments later, the wind swept the bike from beneath me, sending me crashing onto the ice.

The only way I could keep hold of my bike was to attach it to a loop on my boot, but even so, it was a struggle to keep both the bike and me upright. I battled constantly with my balance. The visibility dropped, and I could only just make out my front wheel in the blizzard. The snow fell in horizontal sheets, I was disorientated, and it wasn't easy to figure out the way ahead or where I had come from.

I tried to use the wind as my indicator, but the south-westerlies were now combined with whirling gusts from every direction. The temperature dropped to minus 30 degrees Celsius. I knew I couldn't stop as I'd be unable to put more kit on before I froze to death, let alone erect a tent. I was down to two kilometres per hour, tugging my bike along, desperately trying not to let go of it, as riding it was now out of the question. I was shocked at how fast the storm hit. I would have put my tent up and sat out the worst if I had more warning. I panicked as sweat and tears poured down my face. I had only one option. I had to keep going.

For two and a half hours, I battled the frigid, polar-like conditions, at times pedalling my bike, at others pushing it, while continuously reminding myself, "Be strong... Be strong... Be strong." I had not eaten or drunk for a while, and it was beginning to show as my body was weakening against the incessant gusts. It was taking all my strength to stay upright. A massive gust whipped me off my bike, and I landed with a thump on my back and head. I lay for a few seconds before the shivers began, and I forced myself up on my feet, tethering myself to the bike with a bungee cord.

Then a miracle happened; like coming out of a bad dream, I noticed large mounds of snow appearing ahead of me. The whiteout was beginning to lift. As though by magic, in a matter of a few minutes, the wind dropped, the snow stopped falling, and a small section of blue sky lit up my world. The storm had abated as quickly as it had arrived.

I was still 300 kilometres from the finish line, but in my mind, I had made it. I'd weathered the storm. My body stood strong, and my mind carried me through the worst conditions I had ever faced. My overriding question was how on earth I would cope if weather conditions were even worse at the South Pole.

That night, inside my tent, I treated myself to plenty of freeze-dried rations, spaghetti Bolognese, chocolate chip pudding and whey protein powder to try and rebuild my battered, bruised body. My trousers felt tight, and it was difficult to remove my jacket. My left hip and elbow had swollen into tight, shiny mounds of flesh, so for the next two days, I lived on extra strong painkillers, way beyond the recommended dosage, but it helped to dull the pain. It was only when I returned home and visited the doctor with my still swollen elbow that I was told,

"Maria, you've fractured the bone."

The next day I was greeted with over a foot of snow, and the ice road that supposedly ran along the western shoreline a few days earlier was completely buried. As I struggled through the snow, I came across a truck trying to adopt the same idea that Matt had a few days earlier of building an ice ramp to ride over a chasm in the ice. The driver reversed at an amazing speed, and then, with full throttle and snow spraying everywhere, he charged for the opening in the ice and cleared it with ease, leaving the ground by a good metre. "These Russians are crazy but brave!" I thought. I later discovered the sobering truth that hundreds of vehicles lay submerged at the bottom of Lake Baikal.

The snow layer on top of the ice deepened, but the jellybeans and liquorice stored in my bum bag kept my motivation high. By now, I was so drugged up with glucose that my injuries were bothering me less, and, for the first time on the journey, I took note of my surroundings. The Baikal Mountains rose steeply over the lake's northwestern shore, densely wooded with a combination of Grey Alder, Aspen, Downy Birch, Scots Pine, and Siberian Spruce. The highest peak, Chersky Mountain, towered at 2,572 metres, and the snow on its ridges glistened against the bright blue sky. The light breeze was sufficient to create a sharp crispness in the air. I donned my balaclava for extra protection. A nearby river that fed the lake was frozen in time, a gentle landslide marking its passage through the trees. I felt a magical moment encompass me as I cycled along—a tiny spec on this frozen giant of a lake over 7,000 miles from home.

These special moments seem unobtainable during the humdrum of everyday life, yet out here, fighting for survival, they are like tiny miracles that help speed me on my way. They are even more poignant after a tough episode, and I am forever thanking my lucky stars for still being here to tell the story.

The track I was following wound in and out from the coastline. Due to the deep snow, I could only ride part of the way. It was impossible to pedal my bike through it. I realised that fatter tyres wouldn't have helped in soft, snowy conditions. There was no escaping from the fundamental fact that once you drop below a certain speed, the bike's stability goes, and you end up putting a foot down.

My research had shown that snow in Antarctica was very different to elsewhere in the world and tended to solidify firmly into a surface crust due to very low temperatures and lack of atmospheric moisture. Fat bikes were heavy and, with the extra weight of kit, require superhuman power to stay upright. I had tested a few fat bikes earlier in the year, and now, seeing for myself how Matt and Jez had struggled just as much as I had in deep, soft snow on a regular mountain bike, I was rapidly going off the idea of using a one for my South Pole expedition.

It was disheartening to ride for 30 minutes and find that I was only two kilometres closer to the finish, even though I had covered seven kilometres. Travelling in a straight line was impossible. I was battling regularly through mounds of ice and snow, trying to avoid the inevitable chasms that would suck me into the depths of the lake.

Towards the end of the day, it was no longer possible to even push my bike through the snow, so I hooked it up over my right shoulder and staggered through the thigh-deep snow, dragging one foot after the other.

On my last day, an unexpected challenge awaited me: the finish line was nowhere to be found. After entering the shoreline side of Severobaykalsk and climbing through someone's back garden, I saw the finish flags at the lake's edge. I had completed the race, but there was no sign of the organisers. After such a life-threatening experience, it was a bitter disappointment. My sense of abandonment lessened when locals from a nearby wooden caravan kindly invited me in and offered me the most comforting tea and biscuits I had ever enjoyed. I even drew my first laughter throughout my stay in Russia by showing them how my long, neglected hair could stand on end after seven days without care. I must have looked like a freak show, but my odd display worked. Suddenly, with smiles and claps, we were friends.

The organisers turned up an hour later. They had been dealing with competitors who had suffered death-defying experiences on the lake. Only eight competitors, including Matt, Jez, and me, out of thirty starters, completed the race. I was the first female home and second overall to the Russian cycle-cross champion. Due to the extreme conditions and near fatalities, the race was never run again.

After the race, a few other finishers and I camped on the race organiser's cabin floor, including my new friends Matt and Jez, to await our train back to Irkutsk. The cabin stood close to a row of tumbledown shacks on stilts that bordered Lake Baikal. One of the organisers, John, broke the news that the Spanish competitor had fallen through the ice on the first day. Hearing this shocked everyone, and I felt the cabin walls closing in on me.

"We were lucky that he was an experienced racer, and he had his poles at the ready, which allowed him to pull himself out of the ice," said John. "He was wet and freezing, of course, so he ran for five hours to the edge of the lake, where he collected wood to make a fire to dry off. Thankfully, it saved his life." I said a prayer to myself for my fortunate survival.

I waited impatiently in Severobaykalsk for three days for my train back to Irkutsk. My daily forays into Severobaykalsk, a short distance from the lake in search of food and communication opportunities, were depressing. However, I was delighted to find a fresh pair of knickers on a ramshackle market stall. The town was full of towering, oppressive, prefabricated buildings where people dressed in brown, black and grey passed by like impenetrable shadows with little expression. It created a mood of monotony, which made me long for the vibrancy of life back home in the UK. Located on a plateau at the northern end of Lake Baikal, Severobaykalsk was not a place I wished to return to.

I heaved my bike and bags onto the Trans-Siberian train. I was ushered immediately into a cramped carriage by an expressionless guard for the 36-hour journey across the barren wilderness of Russia. Thank goodness I had survived, and I was on my way home from one of the most dangerous experiences of my life. I wondered how much worse conditions would be at the South Pole. Would the ice be cracking under my tyres? How likely would it be for me to fall into a crevasse, and would I be able to climb out? Cycling in deep snow had been impossible, so I either had to pray that there would be no deep snow or significantly modify my bike design. I wondered how long the knee pain I had experienced on the third day of the race would take to heal up. I could still feel it with every movement I made. I prayed that I had not done any permanent damage that could jeopardise my expedition to Antarctica, where the distances would be far greater.

I was joined in the small, stiflingly hot train compartment by a tall Russian businessman with a square face and a moustache carrying a briefcase. To my surprise, he climbed over my bike and immediately started to undress. He whipped off his tie, shirt and trousers to reveal woolly thermals and mohair slippers. He turned to me, gesticulating that the bike squashed into the centre of the cabin was a problem. Without giving me a chance to communicate with him, and before I could intervene, he grabbed my bike by the rear brake cable and prised it into the overhead locker above the door with the handlebars and front wheels hanging out. Next, he reached for my large red 65-litre dry bag that had been the contents of my home for the last week and practically drop-kicked it underneath one of the bunks. By the look on his face, I wouldn't have been surprised if he had hurled it out of the window.

Apparently satisfied with his achievement, he cracked open a bottle of beer and started playing games on his mobile phone. I tried occasionally to make eye contact with him, but he ignored my invitations. It was going to be a long, hot, uncommunicative journey. Outside the train window, it was minus 30 degrees Celsius, but inside, the cabin had been heated to a blistering plus 25 degrees. I had only been on board for a short time, but I was already stifling hot, sweating through the thermals I had been racing in for seven days. I rested back uncomfortably on the top bunk of our four-bunk compartment.

The seven days I spent on the ice of Lake Baikal and preparing for this race had been a massive learning curve. It had been dangerous, painful, and scary but amazing. Most importantly, it proved perfect training for my planned expedition to Antarctica. It had fuelled a passion within me.

My thoughts were interrupted by the appearance of a second businessman in our compartment. He completed the same ritual as the first, and being even larger in stature, he revealed even baggier thermals and stripy slippers. He climbed into his bunk and immediately began to snore, which practically shook the carriage. The train rolled on, and it was too late for me to escape. My exercise-induced cough proved useful in intermittently arresting his snoring. I giggled over the Trans-Siberian marketing flyer that read 'Discover the romance of Russia with an epic Trans-Siberian rail trip.' Epic it was turning out to be. Romantic, definitely not!

Every thirty minutes during the journey, I climbed down from my bunk and escaped to the gangway linked to the adjoining carriage to breathe fresh air. It was completely open, cold and rattling, and I gazed out at the harsh Siberian winter and endless snow-clad forests that flashed past through the open sides of the train. This was where the smokers gathered in their heavy, furry Russian coats and hats, and they looked at me with dour expressions as I used the opportunity to cool down from the sauna experience in my carriage. I was wearing my polar boots outside and going barefoot in the carriage, neither of which seemed to conform to Russian etiquette. Perhaps I should pack some dog-chewed brown slippers next time. There were no refreshments available on the train, only a hot water tap where, fortunately, I could rehydrate some of my leftover freeze-dried rations to sustain me on this laborious journey.

15 hours later, we had our first prolonged stop of two hours. The train journey had been sluggish and had not exceeded 38 kilometres

per hour. I told myself I would have been better off cycling at my peak fitness. It was time to head out, stretch my legs, and escape the stuffy train. I donned my warm clothes and stepped out into the snow. Breathing in the ice-cold air was a relief, which calmed my sweaty body. I crossed the bridge over the track and found a small cafe where I bought a bacon salad and some chocolate. After walking around the grey, barren station, I decided to play it safe and return to my train. To my horror, my carriage and all the following carriages had disappeared, leaving just six of the original twelve-carriage train.

My frantic sign language to a prim station guard led to nothing, and I was left on the platform in a state of panic. Then, out of the corner of my eye, I spotted the shady figure of one of my former carriage companions in the distance at the end of the platform. Instinctively, I ran after him down the platform. Even though we had not spoken, he seemed to be the friendliest figure around. As he approached the end of the platform, he jumped down onto the track and crossed over another six railway lines. I followed him swiftly, without question. Thankfully, he led me straight to our carriage and the rest of the train that had been split from the other section and re-routed to a different platform. Very relieved, I climbed on board and was reunited with my sauna-like carriage, where I stayed for the rest of the journey, mulling over the amazing experience I had had cycling the length of Lake Baikal.

# 7. The Design of the Polar Cycle

"Surround yourself with people who want to help
unconditionally"

After my experience in Siberia, I finally accepted that biking in soft, deep snow was practically impossible, particularly with a heavy load. I needed a more snow-friendly cycle and was constantly tweaking new possibilities in search of the perfect bike for the job. I'd tested fat bikes in the past, but apart from having wider, fatter tyres that could run at much lower pressure, the fundamentals were still unsuitable for slower speeds in deep snow.

On Lake Baikal, I battled continuously with the constant strong wind that literally swept me off my bike on numerous occasions. I knew the fierce Antarctic winds could be ten times worse. Matt and Jez had been on fat bikes and experienced the same difficulties I had encountered on my mountain bike. In reality, my mountain bike was significantly more efficient on pure sheet ice. However, understanding that this is a rarity in Antarctica, I recognised the need to focus on my homework seriously. I needed other adaptions, more personal ones, in fact, including making the seat of my bike more comfortable to prevent the very sore bum that I had experienced in Siberia. I also struggled with an earlier elbow injury caused by a ski accident, which was aggravated by the constant pressure of holding myself upright for long periods with my arms on the handlebars, not to mention my fractured elbow and painful knee. It became clear that the bike I would use in Antartica needed radical changes.

I considered whether skis or stabilisers would give me the stability that bikes lacked when travelling at very low speeds in snow, and I began to draft ideas and drawings. I was reluctant about adding skis because I would then be moving further away from a bike and more into the territory of skiing, which was already a proven means of polar travel. The idea behind my expedition was to do things differently and better. I wanted this to be a smart expedition. If I could not come up with a good alternative to skiing, then it would be a pointless exercise. I re-focused my thoughts on the principles of cycling and put the idea of skis behind me.

One afternoon, while searching the internet, I came across a blog written by an Antarctic scientist who was working at the research station at McMurdo on Ross Island. Scrolling down, I picked up the words 'South Pole Traverse' and was intrigued to find out more. Excitedly, I read on to find that this traverse had taken place for the first time in 2003 as a means of delivering fuel overland to the South Pole. The United States National Science Foundation funded it. It was part of a programme to create a lower-cost and potentially more reliable method of supplying the South Pole station with fuel. The chosen route was from the McMurdo station, across the Ross Ice Shelf, up through the Transantarctic Mountain Range and then due south across the Polar Plateau to the South Pole. My mind began bubbling with an array of scenarios; I searched for pictures of the traverse and details of the snow conditions. Would this be a smarter route by bike to the Pole?

I learnt about the crevasse-ridden Ross Ice Shelf, historically known as the Great Ice Barrier. This term aptly captured its role as a formidable physical and psychological barrier to early Antarctic explorers. It is the world's largest floating slab of ice, roughly the size of Spain. Glaciologists had been studying a five-kilometre-wide crevasse field, known as the shear zone, that helped stabilise the Ross Ice Shelf. With their specially designed robots to detect crevasses under the ice, they recorded odd flow patterns that indicated that the shear zone was unstable. As the shear zone was the starting line for the South Pole Traverse, crevasse faults had to be remediated each year before the traverse began.

I could only find one picture of the whole traverse taken from afar as it climbed up through the Transantarctic Mountain Range via the Leverett glacier. I pulled out a large map of Antarctica and scanned the coast for options. Could this be a potential route for me to take?

Wayne's birthday was fast approaching, and we'd planned to head off to celebrate in the Seychelles. He was brought up in the warmth of Southern Africa, and he longed for some winter sun. The day before we were due to leave in November 2012, a Google alert came through on my e-mail saying that a Norwegian adventurer living in America was planning to cycle to the South Pole this year. My heart sank. Would all my planning go to waste? Would this Norwegian snatch the world first title from me and be the first person to cycle to the Pole? I reminisced on how Scott must have felt to find Amundsen's Norwegian flag flying at the South Pole, beating him to his goal by over a month.

I felt totally deflated, packing my bag reluctantly for our holiday. I couldn't believe someone else had the same idea as me. I told myself that with a world full of cyclists, there was bound to be someone else who was after the title, and I was relieved that I had kept my plans a secret for so long. My only focus now was on watching the progress of this cyclist. As the reports came back on the tough going, impossible riding conditions and the low daily mileage my fellow title chaser achieved, it soon became apparent that he would not make it. He had also set off too late in the austral summer, and I knew the last flights out of Antarctica would not wait for him. I followed his blogs intensely. They continued in a negative fashion until he finally announced that he would turn around. The Hercules Inlet route had proved too much for a cycling expedition.

I felt immensely relieved but guilty that his failure had given me renewed hope of achieving the title for myself. Visions of my struggle on Lake Baikal resurfaced, and I felt his stress and disappointment at having to turn back. I became absorbed in the importance of that moment of decision that no one wanted to make. Do you struggle, or do you give in? At what point does your mind give in to the signals that your body has had enough? I knew those moments only too well, but they had been strangely deflected by a brief period of disconnection from the decision-making, an interlude of solitude, like a brief rest in a race, which seemed to re-ignite the spark and strengthen me with a strong desire to carry on. My determination and a large helping of luck had overcome moments of terror during adventure races.

With the news that this cherished cycling title was still to be claimed, my state of mind improved, and I could now focus on our holiday. We returned home shortly before Christmas, and as always, Christmas with my family was a treasured time of year. The whole family was together. We joked about the compulsory rhymes that we had struggled to write on our Christmas gifts that had to be deciphered before we could rip off the wrapping paper, and we ate and drank well into the night. My sister's two children, Luca and Anya, whom I secretly wished were mine, even called me their second mummy.

With Christmas and New Year behind me, I had much to do. I had one year to go and needed a sponsor, so I began listing companies to approach. I also had to finalise my route and, most importantly, sort the bike out. I organised a meeting with Marcus, the owner of Qoroz Titanium Bikes, who had sponsored me over the last few years, his colleague Chris, Wayne, and my father, to begin designing a cycle suitable for my South Pole mission.

We met at the Qoroz office in Chippenham and spent the afternoon discussing options for my uniquely designed cycle. Stability was a huge concern because without it, I'd end up pushing the bike most of the way, and I could hardly class that as a cycling expedition. We considered three or even four wheels as essential to gain this stability. Due to the endless hours I would be sitting in the saddle, my position and comfort on the cycle seat were also vitally important. It was obvious that if I sat with my legs in front of me, it would maximise the aerodynamics, but how would this be to cycle? Maybe it would be a more powerful position as a back support would allow me to use the strength in my legs even more. I could repeatedly push 85 kilograms in the gym in this position, so I knew it was one of my strengths.

We looked at tracked vehicles but ruled them out for being too heavy. I also had to consider that I had to fly everything across the world to begin the expedition. We looked at pictures of other cyclists' homemade contraptions and had a good laugh while picking up some valuable tips. In the end, we decided that three wheels with fat tyres and a recumbent position would be the cycle for the job. All parties accepted the idea, and the vehicle for my expedition was conceived. We named it the Polar Cycle, and the expedition became known as the White Ice Cycle. Marcus and Chris began drawing up the design, but a few days later, I received a panicked call from Marcus saying that while he really wanted to help, he didn't feel his company had the expertise on recumbent three-wheeled cycles. I had only nine months to go, and this was a bitter disappointment.

Fortunately, Marcus had been working on a backup plan. He had found a company in Falmouth that specialised in recumbent trikes, called Inspired Cycle Engineering, and they were keen to be involved in my project. Before I knew it, Marcus, Wayne, and I were heading down to Falmouth in my car.

After four hours of driving, we rolled up at a small, inconspicuous unit on an industrial estate with little sign of life. We jumped out of the car to stretch our legs and hopefully be greeted with coffee and lunch before sitting down to talk business.

Lois, who worked in marketing, opened the door to their unit, and after a brief hello and handshake, we were marched quickly into one of the meeting rooms where Neil, one of the company's owners, and two designers sat around the table. We delved directly into the technical details of the Polar Cycle. I had drawn up a user specification document explaining the fat tyres and the need for ultra-low gears to tackle the steep gradient of the Transantarctic Mountain Range, as this was currently my preferred route. Traction was vital; the rear wheel needed to be as far underneath me as possible to produce this. I also needed to fit ice studs in the tyres, particularly for the steep terrain. The team, minus the joint owner Chris, was delighted to be involved in a world-first expedition, and discussions went well.

It was then time for me to test one of their existing trikes. I jumped into the saddle and flew off up the road. The position was very comfortable, but being so close to the road was unnerving, especially when giant trucks zoomed past en route to deliver products to the nearby units. Cycling up hills was challenging, but it suited me as more leg strength and less cardiovascular exertion were required. Downhill was a whole heap of fun, and the aerodynamics were incredible. I was overtaking the delivery drivers.

As I rolled back into the car park, Neil was waiting for me on another trike and led me off down a rough trail through the woods that backed onto the industrial estate. With small regular wheels, the trike was not up to the job, and as I tried to cycle back up an uneven, muddy section, the back wheel just spun. It reconfirmed that I would need as much weight over the back wheel as possible. Carrying heavy kit on a rear frame could be beneficial, which would cancel the need for a sledge. This was a relief as the dynamics of towing a sledge had been my big concern.

With my trial run complete, we shook hands and agreed that they would begin to work on the project and that I would have a prototype within three months. In the meantime, they provided me with one of their trikes so I could get used to sitting in a recumbent position. It was the first time I had cycled a trike. This became an absolute pleasure as I was developing stronger legs, and with less cardiovascular activity, my heart rate rarely rose above 120 beats per minute—the equivalent of a brisk walk. It was a great formula for an endurance expedition.

It was now May; time was ticking by, and I had a busy season of Burn Series sporting events to organise. I had so much to do and so little time. In between organising events, I spent my days contacting potential sponsors. It was a frustrating task, mainly because it was difficult to elicit honest responses. I would far rather have an outright 'no' as opposed to those who kept me hanging on or didn't even respond. I quickly acquired a catalogue of common responses, and it went like this: 'Sounds totally amazing!' translated as 'I don't believe you can possibly do that.'

'I hope you have a wonderful time' translated as 'you are totally mad to even think about it.'

'Sorry, but our budget is fully allocated' translated as 'even if we had some money, we wouldn't give it to you as we don't believe you can do it.' 'Good luck to you' translated as 'we'll be watching when you fail!'

The most difficult replies to deal with were those along the lines of 'Oh, maybe, let me talk to the team.' Sometimes, I was strung along for months. I persisted with a five-call rule, which meant I would give up after five phone calls or messages. On one occasion, I found out that the lady I had been calling repeatedly was on maternity leave, so instead, I spoke to her stand-in, who sounded interested and even began to talk figures. Again, I was strung along for months before a final negative reply. I worked from a spreadsheet that listed 168 companies, some local, some national, and those with a sporting connection. My Excel spreadsheet gradually turned from green to red as the 'no's' flooded in.

Sadly, I had to accept that I didn't have the fame of a pop star or well-known personality; I was just an ordinary British woman with an ambition to succeed. The emotional turmoil of trying to find a sponsor was exhausting.

I was reminded of some poignant words I'd read at the end of Apsley Cherry-Garrard's book, The Worst Journey in the World, reflecting on his experiences with Captain Scott's 1910-1913 Terra Nova Expedition:

"And I tell you if you have the desire for knowledge and the power to give it physical expression, go out and explore. If you are a brave man, you will do nothing: if you are fearful, you may do much, for none but cowards have need to prove their bravery. Some will tell you that you are mad, and nearly all will say: 'What is the use?' For we are a nation of shopkeepers, and no shopkeeper will look at research which does not promise him a financial return within a year. And so, you will sledge nearly alone, but those with whom you sledge will not be shopkeepers: that is worth a good deal. If you march your Winter Journeys, you will have your reward..."

Aside from financial rewards, my preparations and research enabled me to meet a few, but definitely special, like-minded people and on the positive side, I enjoyed a wide range of consolation prizes in the form of all the kit and equipment I needed for the expedition.

Life was hectic. I was training for three to four hours every day, and I still had to finalise my route and coordinate the logistics. If I was going to start my expedition on the Ross Ice Shelf, how would I get there? To charter a flight would cost 250,000 euros, which was totally out of the question. The problem was that my preferred route was virtually untouched by other expeditions favouring the logistically accessible Hercules Inlet route.

Yet the Ross Ice Shelf served as the starting point for some of the most iconic expeditions of all time, including Scott's ill-fated Terra Nova Expedition to the Pole in 1910-1913, Amundsen's successful South Pole expedition in 1911, and Shackleton's furthest south expedition during the Nimrod Expedition of 1907-1909. I wanted to experience the Transantarctic Mountain Range, Earth's most inaccessible mountain range.

These mountains form a colossal 3,500-kilometre spine dividing East Antarctica from West Antarctica. Shackleton first found a route through the mountains onto the Polar Plateau by discovering the Beardmore Glacier. Scott climbed the Beardmore, Amundsen, the Axel Heiberg Glacier and I would climb the Leverett Glacier. Leverett was ninety kilometres long and seven kilometres wide and named after an eminent American glacial geologist called Frank Leverett. I knew little about glaciers, but my research told me they were formed when snow remained in the same location over many years and compressed into large, thickened ice masses. Due to their sheer mass, glaciers flow like languid rivers and currently occupy about ten per cent of the world's total land area, with most located in Antarctica. Fortunately, such movement was imperceptible to the human eye.

While searching through some of my Lake Baikal photographs, I stumbled across a picture from the Adventure Awards in London that I attended in the summer of 2012. At these awards, I was presented with a beautiful glass trophy for my Siberian Black Ice Race achievement. After giving a very impromptu and slightly embarrassing thank you speech in front of 500 guests, a bit haphazard due to my intoxication and lack of preparation, I met a man from Iceland who worked for a truck company. His firm had provided trucks for the Top Gear programme at the North Pole in 2007. Could they help me with transport in Antarctica? This connection proved one of the most useful

I had made to date.

I contacted Emil, the CEO of Arctic Trucks and told him about my plans. His advice and encouragement strengthened my conviction that my planning was going along the right lines. Arctic Trucks were experts in polar travel, and I really wanted to work with them. It was to prove a great relationship.

It was spring 2013, and I planned to set off in December 2013, yet I had no cycle, no confirmed route, no flights, no idea if I was fit enough and only £20,000 in savings, which was being sucked up by my business. The expedition costs could total over five times that amount, and I didn't know how I was going to raise it. What I did have, though, was determination, a very supportive and close family and the makings of a great expedition team. When I felt low, I put myself through three hours of physical exercise to focus my mind. It worked a treat as every time I came back fighting harder.

The strain of these inevitable highs and lows was showing in our relationship, and when Wayne accused me of being selfish, I felt very hurt. Was I really being selfish, or was I just focused? I thought of my mother, the least selfish person I know, and how she taught me to respect other peoples' feelings and always consider them in all situations. Maybe I hadn't yet mastered this technique. I felt sad, but deep down, I knew Wayne was just concerned about what I was about to embark on, and it was probably his way of telling me this.

The logistics of the expedition were becoming more complicated by the day. Arctic Trucks were now playing a pivotal role in my planning. They talked me through their plans for the season in Antarctica as we tried to figure out at what point I could fit into their schedule. They supported the Walking with the Wounded expedition, which would see four teams of injured service men and women ski to the South Pole. Among them would be Prince Harry and heartthrob actor Alexander Skärsgård. My sister, who over the last year had distanced herself from me, trying to figure out why I wanted to put myself through the trauma of cycling to the South Pole, soon showed a little more interest at the mention of Alexander Skärsgård. I, on the other hand, had to Google who he was!

Arctic Trucks would finish their support for the Walking with the Wounded expedition at the South Pole around December 15, so if I could get there in time, they could drive me to the Ross Ice Shelf from where I would begin my expedition. I promptly started discussions with the expedition's leader, Ed Parker, to see if I could use their inbound flight to reach the South Pole. He was delighted to offset some of the cost, and we agreed on £15,000 for a seat. I knew it was going to a very good cause as well as helping me take a step closer to the start of my expedition so I was delighted.

To add to the complex logistics, this flight did not leave from the main ALE expedition base in Antarctica at Union Glacier, which I'd been expecting to fly into. Instead, I had to reach the Russian airbase, Novolazarevskaya, situated at the Schirmacher Oasis in Queen Maud Land. This was about as far away from the Ross Ice Shelf as it could be. It was from here that the Walking with the Wounded inbound flight would leave for the South Pole. This was the flight I needed to be on. The complexity of the logistics was growing by the day.

After further discussions with Emil, I contacted a company called Antarctic Logistics Centre International, which operated flights from Cape Town in South Africa to Novolazarevskaya Station for scientists and staff. I began conversations with a friendly German voice belonging to Anne. After becoming stuck in the middle of a logistical debate between Anne and Emil for two months, we finally agreed on a master plan that would get me to the Ross Ice Shelf and my starting point. After my expedition, my return plan was to be transported by truck from the South Pole along the Hercules Inlet route and back towards Union Glacier, from where I would fly out with Adventure Networks International to Chile, South America.

I made a conscious decision not to worry about the return journey because, at this stage, just planning the journey to my start line was a complex logistical operation. While I thrived on the complexity of the planning because it was yet another obstacle to cross, I was also aware that it could all go horribly wrong at the last minute. Flights in and out of Antarctica were only ever confirmed on the actual day of departure. All my planning was literally in the hands of the weather.

The constant doubt that came with doing something no one had ever succeeded in before and whether I would be able financially to get this ground-breaking Antarctica expedition off the ground was a daily struggle. The fear I experienced on Lake Baikal made me realise that I could never control nature. My father's warnings echoed in my mind as he recounted the story of one of his best friends falling through ice in a lake in Sweden. It made me realise that I had been too close to death on that Siberian expedition. I needed to make this a story of extraordinary success, not a tragedy.

The afternoon my Polar Cycle finally arrived at my home in Wales was a huge milestone in the expedition planning. As we lifted it from the back of Chris's van, I was shocked at the size of it. It measured not far off a metre wide and two metres long. Unlike most trikes, the three fat tyres, two at the front and one at the back were imposing. There seemed to be endless amounts of chain, two separate chains in fact, and the rack suspended over the rear wheel looked like it could carry a house. It seemed unreal. I was eager to test it in harsh conditions.

We put it back in the van and drove to the nearby dunes at Merthyr Mawr to test it on the most challenging local terrain possible. I managed to cycle up a dune with Chris, weighing 90 kilograms on the back and deemed the Polar Cycle a great success, at least for now. It wasn't perfect and required a few tweaks and changes over the next few months, which ICE obligingly carried out. The real test ahead was how it would perform on snow and ice.

# 8. A Tough Training Regime

"Achieve first and talk about it later"

I can't wait for all this to be over," Wayne moaned sleepily as I climbed out of bed to the sound of the alarm at 5 am. I joked briefly about how staying in bed would not earn me a world record. I pulled on my cycling clothes, wishing I could melt back under the warm covers, but it was time for my daily grind to begin.

Training was now at the top of the list, and I needed an early start to ensure I hit my training targets. My morning began with a two to three-hour Polar Cycle ride, often around the deer park. The idea behind this stint was to clock up the miles and strengthen my leg muscles to become accustomed to the endless hours of cycling ahead of me in Antarctica. It was also a means of deprivation training.

There may be times in Antarctica when I would have to ration food and water, and I needed to know how my body would perform when deprived of food. Against common practice, I purposely trained on an empty stomach without food or fluids to test out that I could still perform by getting my body used to this feeling of all-around deprivation. This was not easy; my thigh muscles strained and tingled with effort, and I produced little power and plenty of frustrated cycling during the first weeks of my training programme. But my body soon began to adapt and understand that it needed to work despite a low energy supply. I was training my body to learn.

My tough training and expedition experience taught me surprising details about my body's survival ability. I began to get used to the feeling of being totally drained and I learnt to appreciate how nutrition helped me to perform. It made me realise how amazing a woman's body is. The process of childbirth is just one example of how a woman's pain threshold is naturally high and that mothers are conditioned to put their child's needs for warmth and nutrition before their own. As child-bearers, women are made to withstand deprivation and endurance, and in difficult circumstances, they can cope with far fewer supplies. I also learnt that regardless of gender, the power of the mind can do incredible things, and I was much more capable than I thought. At times, my mind was my worst monster.

Light relief came after my training session when I would eat a large, overdue breakfast, including porridge topped with seeds, goji berries, banana and cranberries, a boiled egg and bagel and copious amounts of herbal tea and water. This was followed by lunch a few hours later. I didn't follow a special diet and didn't deprive myself of any foods. I just ate what I felt in the amounts I felt I needed until my appetite was satisfied. My body became my dietician.

My evening training session alternated between sprint sessions on foot or on a gym bike and an endurance ride on my road or mountain bike. The sprint sessions were always tough because my 'slow twitch' muscle fibres, needed for endurance, found it an alien experience. Still, I pushed myself hard with forty-five-minute interval sprints, and as the weeks passed, I became stronger, faster and tougher and could endure longer sprint sessions. I rigorously stuck to my painful programme and monitored every training session in infinite detail. Working on my sprint sessions was important as this would enable me to push myself harder during my endurance sessions. The endurance sessions were about clocking up the miles as I pushed my target even further, and I gained huge satisfaction from analysing the results and seeing the improvement.

My days were long and tiring, and I regularly returned from training sessions utterly exhausted. I was physically and mentally tired from cycling, expedition planning, and organising Burn Series events. Much of this organisation required desk time and phone calls, so I devised a cunning plan to combine this sitting-down time with training. I decided to build a desktop that would bridge across the tyres of the Polar Cycle.

Initially, it wasn't the best-designed desk because the plank of wood I had balanced across the front two wheels of the Polar Cycle was too low. My knees constantly hit the plank, so I added an extra feature by raising the plank using two large flowerpots balanced on the wheels. With the Polar Cycle set up on a turbo trainer to create a static cycle, I found I could train and work simultaneously. It looked ridiculous, but it worked brilliantly. From now on, I had not only been doing three hours of focused endurance training per day, but thanks to my cycle desk, managed to sustain endurance training pretty much all day long.

I set up the Polar Cycle in the utility room of my parent's home, but I soon moved it to a covered area outside on the decking so I could occasionally gaze out across the field and see the deer grazing and the calves bouncing through the bracken. I imagined being as fleet of foot as they were, running effortlessly. I imagined my legs were as nimble and light as theirs as I pushed hard against the pedals in a constant rotation. It was approaching summer, and my new workstation was a success, besides the occasional breeze interfering with my paperwork.

Although I had managed to roll work and training together for part of the day, I didn't have time for a social life, so I emailed my friends and apologised for being so elusive.

I took a day off to visit Wayne's friend, who owned a large freezer storage warehouse in Portsmouth and kindly allowed me to cycle around his facility for the day. I wanted to check on the endurance quality of the aircraft-graded steel of the Polar Cycle. I also needed to check that the layering principles for my newly acquired polar clothing were correct and that I wouldn't suffer from any chafing. It also created a perfect opportunity for ITV Wales, who eagerly filmed my every move for a documentary about my expedition.

It felt very odd to circle around the floor-to-ceiling shelves in the giant warehouse stocked with Bernard Matthews turkey twizzlers and Captain Birds Eye fish fingers. The staff who were stacking the shelves must have thought it even odder. After steering around the ends of the racks at speed and nearly knocking a shelf load of frozen peas to the ground, I decided it would be safer to set up my turbo-trainer in a corner of the warehouse.

After a day's stint in the minus 19 degrees Celsius storeroom, I decided on an additional modification to the Polar Cycle. I would ask ICE to lower the pedal shaft as I wanted my feet to be as low as possible to encourage circulation to my most vulnerable parts. In the colder temperatures and with the pressure of my gigantic polar boots, I knew my blood would not flow as well as needed in my seated position. It was important to know that I was pedalling in the most efficient way. Fortunately, Wayne put me in touch with Phil, a previous work colleague and biomechanic, who came to check on my body position on the Polar Cycle. I knew from Lake Baikal that my right kneecap tended to fall inwards as I pedalled, which caused me pain.

After Phil confirmed my problem, he built up the inside of the pedal to help align my knee. His last words were, "It should help, but I am warning you that after plenty of exertion, your knee is going to hurt."

In June, I visited Loughborough University, known for its sporting excellence, for an in-depth physical testing examination. I'd managed to set this up as a consolation prize from Gatorade, who were unwilling to sponsor me financially. This was fitness testing on a rigorous scale with various tests for heart health, lung strength, muscle strength, reaction time, flexibility, power, nutritional awareness and mental strength. It really was the full package.

Dr James Carter, the Gatorade Sports Science Institute lead practitioner, met me at the Loughborough laboratory, along with his colleague Rebecca Randell, who turned my body into a statistical package over the next four hours. James and Rebecca were incredibly physically fit and oozed knowledge about the fitness and nutrition industry. I felt quite the amateur with my self-created theories of fitness and nutrition, but I still found the need to debate with them some of the theories I had about my own body.

On arrival, I was asked to strip off to be weighed. The assessment room was set up with an array of components for monitoring the body. I'd been on starvation since 11 pm the night before, and now, at 12 midday, thirteen hours had passed since I had last eaten; I stepped onto the scales and closed my eyes, hoping that when I opened them, I'd be delighted to see a weight reading below what I was expecting. It read 64.614 kilograms. This was the first time I'd had an accurate reading of my weight, and although I had a relatively slim physique, I was in the lower half of the national average for athletes.

I dressed quickly as James and Rebecca re-entered the room and wired me up to the body composition monitor for an automatic reading. A manual reading followed, which involved highly personal fat-grabbing and fat-shaking techniques used to determine body fat ratios. Apologising as she pulled at my rolls, Rebecca took measurements from my arms, torso and legs. My 'bingo wings,' otherwise known as triceps, belly and 'back of the sides,' a name that my sister and I had developed for the flabby bits that hang over the back of jeans, were all exposed to rigorous testing.

It was an uncomfortable experience because the skin callipers used meant that Rebecca needed to grab not just my skin but also the layer of fat that sat under it. In certain places on the body, such as my thighs, she would grab the skin, fat and muscle and then need to shake off the muscle to get the correct reading for the fat. My dignity had left the room by now. I tried to comfort myself with the knowledge that they were professionals and did this every day. As a qualified personal trainer, I'd used this tool on others. This time, I tasted some of my own medicine. It was most unpleasant, but it produced some delightful results and a good few percentages less than the reading from the body composition monitor, which Rebecca used to ensure accuracy.

I received readings of my bone mass, muscle and body fat percentage, broken down into limb and water levels. I was moved swiftly onto the X-ray machine, which again differentiated between bone, fat, muscle and water. For this, I had to lie on a bed with a foam brick pressed up against my thighs and in between my ankles to ensure I was correctly aligned. It took about fifteen minutes for the scan to complete, and following that, I was on to the final body composition test, which did add insult to injury.

The 'Bod Pod' test uses radiation, so I had to take a quick pregnancy test first, which thankfully proved negative. As James and Rebecca took readings, I was told to sit in my bra and pants, wearing a hat like a swim cap with my hands on my knees. During my second visit to the facility just before leaving for Antarctica, it was even more difficult to keep a straight face during this test as the ITV Wales cameraman was filming me through the panels.

With the body composition testing complete, I was kept in suspense about the results as I was moved on to the next test, where I was about to get very sweaty. The VO2 Max Testing is regarded as a controversial test by the fitness industry, and personally, I've never been a firm believer in it as a tool for making improvements. It's more about measuring potential. The idea behind the VO2 Max test was to push me to 100% of my heart rate to see how I dealt with oxygen circulation around my body. I had to cycle until I almost fell off the bike with sheer exhaustion. The test took twenty-two minutes to complete, and I began by pedalling at 60 watts. This was increased by 30 watts every three minutes. I managed to cycle up to three hundred and 60 watts before collapsing in a heap.

During the test, I wore a face mask that measured the amount of oxygen I had inhaled and the amount of carbon dioxide I had exhaled. My mask filled quickly with sweat and snot as I struggled to keep pedalling. It was not a pleasant sight. As soon as the test was over, with snot pouring down my face, James took me aside and extracted copious amounts of blood from my arm to measure my body's ability to burn fat. The theory is that the quicker the body can switch from burning available carbohydrates from food to burning fat, the higher the endurance level.

At last, it was time for some controlled physical rest while I sat and completed numerous questionnaires about my lifestyle and eating habits. This was followed by two different reaction time tests measuring my overall body reaction time and hand-eye coordination. I must admit they made me look like a rather un-coordinated monkey! My long limbs just wouldn't respond with the swiftness or agility required of them.

After this mammoth series of testing, the conclusion was that I needed to develop stronger legs, improve my body's ability to burn fat and spend as much time cycling as possible. James and Rebecca gave me some excellent guidance on my current training programme to help make it more efficient. I was excited about the prospect of building my fitness further and seeing an improvement, so I left with a renewed focus. My next visit to the Loughborough fitness facility was scheduled for the end of November, two weeks before leaving for Antarctica. By that date, I planned to be super fit.

Wayne could see how important my training was to me, and he stuck by my side for the most part, yet some underlying issues had been left unsaid or said in haste. I was concerned that my focus was going to ruin us. Wayne had been through a challenging year with the part sale of his business. It had put a tremendous amount of stress on his shoulders. Our fiery exchanges never lasted long but left us both turning our backs on each other as we refused to understand each other's viewpoints. It again demonstrated that we were stubborn, focused, and determined, but would this bode for a lasting relationship? We were now living in an apartment overlooking Cardiff Bay where there was little room for my work, his work, and my expedition planning to all live happily together.

As my training progressed, I marvelled at how clever the human body was and how a string of individual variables prevented the creation of a formula for sporting performance. I found that my body went through a process of rapid change, to begin with, and then it reached a plateau in which body weight and fitness levels remained constant; in other words, my body resisted improvement. As this happened at different times for every person, I realised there was no one answer for everyone. Sports science could never be exact because the body was so individual.

To stimulate my body from this inevitable plateau, I introduced 'cheat days' when I did no sport and ate as much calorific food as possible. I decided this was the best way to coax my body out of thinking it knew what I was trying to do to it: make it fitter and leaner. I needed to learn about my body in infinite detail and calculate my own variables. I found no magical solution to fitness and weight loss; it was all about knowing my body. I could then develop a personal eating and exercise plan.

I found that calorie counting helped, provided it involved a balanced diet, but I avoided diets that were strict on no fat, sugar or carbohydrates since I found they created short-term and potentially harmful outcomes. Despite my rigorous training schedule, I still needed to balance the amount I ate with the energy I expended.

I was 5ft 10 inches tall, weighed 64 kilograms, and had a medium-sized frame for my height. Over the years, I'd learnt that in order not to lose weight or put on weight and at the same time maintain a good level of fitness, I needed to eat 2,200 calories per day. I also felt good if I ate healthy food, as my body had everything needed to recover and feel strong and energised. If I ate unhealthy food, I lacked energy, my skin suffered, and I was far more prone to injuries because my body had not been given sufficient sustenance to recover.

I often reflected on Oscar Wilde's famous saying, 'Everything in moderation, including moderation,' which resonated with me in so many ways. My personal formula was always to make sure I ate a little of everything...even chocolate.

When I raced across the Sahara Desert in the Marathon Des Sables of 2007, I learnt much about my body and its magical ability to store fat innately. Why did I take on such a challenge? At the time, the answer was simple. In my office job as a consultant, I worked late into the evening, spending most of my time at my desk or in the board room. What was left of the evening was spent eating out in restaurants, the inevitable three-course meals and a good helping of wine. This left little time for exercise or recreation, so the pounds began to pile on. When I say that, I was by no means fat, but my girth size was increasing all the time, and in my eyes, I was fat. My clothes felt tight, and I had to walk everywhere, breathing in. Life became uncomfortable as I self-consciously tried to tuck my expanding rolls of fat into my trouser line. I avoided mirrors, I hated the way I looked, and I hated the way I felt. Running across the Sahara Desert seemed like the perfect answer. I had no idea that something as simple as not wanting to be fat would be the driver for some incredible things to follow.

It often amazed me that when I raced with men during expedition adventure races, the weight fell off them after a few days, and they lost precious energy. In contrast, I became stronger as the days went on and had a remarkable ability to store fat when my energy ran out. I finished the Sahara race weighing the same as when I set off. Even running across a desert did not reduce my weight. I concluded that weight loss, in normal day-to-day life, is far more about the food I eat than the exercise I take.

What I eat gives me energy to get through the day, replacing lost essential vitamins and minerals, which are vitally important for body repair while training hard. Other internal organs also need to work efficiently to maintain a healthy heart. I knew that the visceral fat, which is the internal fat in my body that keeps my organs protected and warm, was important, but too much could be dangerous and lead to liver, lung and kidney problems or even a heart attack. I therefore needed to control my fat intake by eating healthy foods and non-saturated fats. I also focused on keeping my organs strong through physical exercise so they could continue to function correctly.

With the recommendations from Loughborough University and my fitness programme in full swing, I needed to plan my nutritional needs before and during the expedition. Unlike in the days when little was known about nutrition and scurvy was a killer, I was now benefiting from a mound of research and advice from umpteen nutritional suppliers keen for me to use their products.

Expedition food is far from appetising, but it contains a balanced amount of everything I need, with up to 800 calories of energy per portion. It is freeze-dried and weighs less than 200 grams per portion. I had a 20-litre pannier bag to accommodate 20 days' worth of food, so the packaging size was also a consideration. I decided to trim off any excess packaging fastidiously.

Sadly, there are few thrills to be gained from this type of nutrition. Even though the mere suggestion of beef stew stimulates my taste buds in normal circumstances, survival rations are predictably bland, which takes the edge off any meal. It is amazing how chicken korma can resemble spaghetti Bolognese so closely.

Interestingly, though, the seemingly small portions are very filling and eating these daily at home would most certainly lead to dramatic weight gain. I discussed with the energy bar manufacturers, 9-bar, about producing some bars with extra lard, though in the end, I decided that this was unnecessary. They were sufficiently calorific for my own needs as they were.

During the next few weeks, I sampled these culinary delights and calculated my nutritional needs for the expedition based on my experimentation. It was vital that I selected correctly to provide plenty of energy and nutrition to see me through the rigours of my Antarctic expedition.

# 9. The Patagonian Last Wild Race

"Competition encourages you to aim high"

Patagonia was a race out of the blue. It all began with a surprise email from adventure racer Neil, who said that the girl in their team had broken her leg and they were desperate for a female replacement. The rules of adventure racing specify a mixed team, and without a female member, they would have been forced to withdraw from the race. There are few female adventure racers in the world and even fewer who race at an international level, so it was a rare opportunity for me. The prospect fired me with excitement, and I couldn't resist the temptation. After all, my fitness levels were good, and this race, coined by fellow world champion racers as the toughest race in the world, was one I should not miss. I also needed a break from the monotony of my training routine for the South Pole.

The Last Wild Race was in two weeks. The sponsor would pay all my expedition costs; I just had to get to the start point. I was fit and loved the prospect of racing in Patagonia, where I had visited with Raleigh International in 2004. Before I knew it, I was part of the Berghaus Adventure Racing team, racing under a German flag.

Travelling to the continent was fraught with difficulties; I missed all my flight connections. After three days of busy airports and virtually no sleep, I felt grouchy even before the race began. Finally, I arrived at the youth hostel in Punta Arenas at 4.30 am, where, to my surprise, my new teammates rolled out of bed to welcome me. There was Neil, a South African runner with six years of adventure racing experience;

Fred, a German triathlete, a few years older who had raced with Neil over the last six years; and Thomas, a mountain leader, also with several years of adventure racing experience. Thomas appeared to be the fittest member of the team.

After this brief greeting, we snatched three hours of sleep until 8 am. My head felt dull and heavy when a tap on the shoulder awoke me to begin a day of race preparation. All I wanted to do was go back to sleep. However, my spirits rose when I met Birgit, our ex-team member, in the morning. Although her leg was in plaster, she was determined to lend her support. She was short and bubbly and an excellent skier and diver who had sadly come to grief during a skiing accident. While I knew I was fit enough for the race, I was apprehensive about working with teammates I did not know. They were strong contenders for the title, which gave me an excitement buzz; at the same time, it increased the pressure on me to do well. The youth hostel was run by a friendly Chilean family, none of whom were over five foot five inches tall, so we all towered over them. Their six-year-old son was intrigued by the amount of kit we had and wanted to be part of our planning. As we laid out our kit to check through the contents, he was always in the way, bombarding us with questions, but I didn't really mind because I had the chance to practice my rusty Spanish.

At first, I felt awkward sitting next to Neil. He was one of those people with personal space boundaries that differed from mine. He was close and touchy, but finding he was the same with everyone was a relief. He always wore his helmet lop-sided due to the GoPro camera that he had attached to one side. Fred was a gentle guy in his late 40s, well-organised and a softie at heart. Thomas was tall, slim and super fit. He was more reserved and a little grumpy, and I never really got to know him. I was delighted that the team immediately took me under their wing.

We spent two days sorting the kit and organising it into transition bags. Over the ten days, we would face ten transition points and seventeen checkpoints, covering 700 kilometres. We needed to pack bags of food, clothes and equipment for each transition point that would see us through until the next transition area. It was a minefield to organise because we had to plan for unexpected phases requiring harnesses and ropes, so we had to carry this extra equipment by bike and on foot, just in case we needed it. We ended up carrying about sixteen kilos of kit each.

We agreed that Neil and Thomas would be the navigators. They were already a pre-formed team, so we decided not to change responsibilities this late in the day. The race start was at Punta Natales, a four-hour bus ride from Punta Arenas. Before we caught the bus, we couldn't resist the temptation of devouring a large 16-inch pizza each, which took us about an hour to eat. We were well and truly full and ready to burn some calories.

We snoozed uncomfortably on the bus that took us to Punta Natales town hall. I waded through a mass of wheels to locate my mountain bike that had been transported on a separate lorry. The official race briefing was at a local restaurant, where we devoured yet another big meal. Then, there were four more hours of kit sorting and a short sleep on a hard floor before it was time to begin.

As midnight struck, eleven determined teams on bikes shot off from Plaza de Armas into the dark, following only the light of their head torches. It was a dangerous start, with plenty of swerving and swaying to avoid the other 43 racers. We soon left the roads of Punta Natales and hit dirt tracks that took us north towards the Torres Del Paine National Park. I was excited about seeing the national park with its mountains, glaciers, lakes and rivers, as I'd only seen them from afar during my previous visit to Chile.

Already, we had lost sight of the world champions, but we could see the Japanese team up ahead, and we were now in third position. Soon after the race started, the rain came down, and as I was not prepared to get wet, I put on my waterproof trousers. Big mistake. I soon realised that cycling with waterproof bottoms hindered me because they slipped down my bottom and restricted my knees as I cycled. It was a schoolgirl error.

After cycling for almost seven hours, the light began to break through to reveal the most magnificent mountain range. This was the Torres del Paine National Park. The sky was ablaze with red streaks from a wild artist's paintbrush, and light, fluffy clouds sailed across the skyline, pierced intermittently by snow-clad mountain tops. It was a breathtaking sight.

We had climbed well above sea level, and the wind had picked up. The five-mile track leading up to the transition area was the most challenging part of the cycle so far. During this stretch, we began to talk about our transition plans. We decided that the boys would focus on taking the bikes apart and putting them away into the transition bags whilst I prepared porridge and our bags for the next phase, a 46-kilometre trek up towards the well-known Horseshoe trail.

We had at least three days ahead of us on foot. This included crossing Glacier Tyndall, one of the largest glaciers in the southern

Patagonian ice field. We began navigating through the forest armed with packets of porridge. The track petered out, and it was now a case of micro navigation. Thomas did a great job of this, and I urged the guys to pick up the pace and begin to jog. I had the Japanese team in my mind and wanted to catch them up.

The sun was shining, painting the scenery in a wide variety of colours that fuelled my excitement. The journey was difficult, manoeuvring through dense forest that stretched endlessly into the distance. A few hours later, the countryside opened, and following a river crossing, we faced a vast grey rocky landscape through which we scrambled up and down ledges, each one more jagged than the last.

The American team had crept up behind us, but there was no sign of the Japanese. The scale of the rocky grey landscape was haunting. After more than 12 hours of racing, we approached the glacier and the second checkpoint, where Birgit, who was helping the organisers, greeted us. We swiped our timing chip and sat down momentarily to put on our crampons. Ahead was the ten-kilometre-wide glacier, which we knew we could not tackle in a straight line because of the crevasses.

As we trekked on, the crevasses became wider, longer and deeper and at one point, I slipped, floundering wildly as I tried to grab the edge of the crevasse. Luckily, Fred, who was just ahead of me, reacted quickly, grabbed my rucksack and pulled me out. It was late afternoon, and unknown to us at this stage, only five teams were left in the race. The others had to retire from the competition after failing to meet the pre-determined time limits.

Unfortunately, the American team overtook us on the glacier, crossing over an extensive range of rivers and crevasses due to a better route selection. As night fell, we took a short nap in the pouring rain on some hard, rocky ground. The discomfort swung us back into action after only a one-and-a-half-hour rest.

The next day our first challenge was a fast-moving torrent of water gushing off the mountains. The river was at least 40 metres wide, so we trekked upstream to find a suitable crossing, but the river only got wider. We had no knowledge of the conditions further down the river as it flowed off around a right-hand bend at a fast speed that would be impossible to swim against. Our only option was to start far enough upstream to ferry glide ourselves across the river before reaching the corner. I was freezing cold, and the thought of crossing the water, only about 10 degrees Celsius, made me shake to my core. I employed the technique of ignoring my feelings and immediately began to strip off, so I was wearing only knickers and my race bib. I tucked everything else in a waterproof bag to preserve it for the other side. I threw my bag over one shoulder and under the other to use it as a float. Out of the corner of my eye, I could see that Neil was following suit, preparing himself for the swim. There was nothing to discuss; we just needed to get to the other side.

I began to walk into the river, and almost immediately, the force of the current threw me off my feet. I started to float uncontrollably at speed, headfirst down the river. I knew I needed to turn my body, so I fought to turn myself on my back to float feet first in what felt like a life-threatening water ride. I began paddling with my right arm to assist my ferry glide, and disaster struck as I repeatedly threw my hand over my head. I had managed to swim out of my bag, and it was heading straight down the river. It contained everything I needed for the expedition, including the maps for days five, six and seven. It was a disaster. I feared I would disappoint everyone as we could not continue without maps. Luckily, Neil had entered the water only a few seconds after me, about ten metres downstream. He was floating down just behind my bag at an amazing speed. He reached to grab hold of it before paddling furiously to assist a ferry glide over to the other side of the river. We all made it to the riverbank, where we lay in a soggy heap, exhausted but fortunately with all our bags. Dripping wet, we gave each other a hug of relief that we had all made it. The shock of our lucky escape left us speechless. We dressed and trekked on.

It wasn't until we followed the river around the corner that we realised we had just missed a huge waterfall with a 40-metre drop scattered with fallen trees. If the drop hadn't killed us, the trees certainly would have.

We arrived at the next checkpoint at the lake's edge before Bend Racing, the American team. Navigation had been vital during this trek, and we'd managed to do a better job of it. I took a moment to gaze at our spectacular surroundings. The glacier that we had just crossed was on our left, with its icy mountain streams pouring out directly into the lake. Intermittently, huge icebergs passed us by to the right. It was surreal, and with sleep deprivation adding to the deception, I felt I was on another planet.

We were given some inflatable kayaks to make the crossing to the other side of the lake, from where we continued our trek through the night. When we could no longer keep our eyes open, we pitched our tent for a short two-hour sleep right next to the Americans on what appeared to be a cliff edge. The Americans proved sharper than us because when their alarms went off, they were up, packed and on their way in a matter of minutes.

The next checkpoint was only a few hours away, and with the cut-offs getting closer, we had to steam on. The morning began to break, and we had another lake to circumnavigate. As the forest was so dense, we decided to trek along the lake's edge in the water, which rose intermittently between ankle and thigh deep. It was bitterly cold, and the icy sensation on my toes was something I would soon regret. Later in the race, I developed a frost nip on my right toe.

We arrived at the next checkpoint and were urged to leave promptly because it was closing in a matter of minutes. We were slowing and in danger of missing the next checkpoint. At times like these, especially when everyone was tired, the team automatically reverted to speaking German, which I only understood a little. I decided I wouldn't let it bother me, and instead, I retreated into my thoughts.

Until now, Thomas had done well on his navigation, but pinpointing where we were started to become more challenging. Due to little sleep, we were all in a trance, and I started to see make-believe tarmac paths, which I wanted to follow, but of course, there was no such thing, only low-hanging branches and straggling roots, which meant every step forward was also a step over. We were tripping and falling, and the terrain became steeper and rockier. The ground fell away steeply to our left, and I now knew why we had been told to carry a climbing rope. In the pitch black, we were fighting through a forest that descended sharply off a cliff edge, and the going became unmanageable. It was pouring with rain, I felt totally lost and sleep-deprived, and I was with three guys I hardly knew in the wilderness of Patagonia. They mumbled together crossly in German. I thought briefly of home and, for a moment, relished in a feeling of total bizarreness as, in a strange way, for a brief few moment, my dramatic experience felt enlightening.

When we could trek no further, Neil took the call to begin an abseil off the cliff edge, and he made a harness out of his rope, which I was reluctant to trust. Four of us would have to risk hanging from a branch in total darkness when we had no idea whether it was strong enough. Yet it seemed our only option. Fred was lowered first to test how far into the blackness we could go. It was difficult to see anything through the pouring rain and darkness. Only a faint glow from our head torches lit up a few metres ahead. After a few nerve-wracking moments, Fred shouted that he had landed on a ledge. Thomas helped me to climb into the makeshift harness, but I panicked as I stared at the branch, which now had my life in its clutches. Thank goodness, I made it to the ledge, but as Neil descended, we heard a crack, and he came thundering down. The branch had given away, but luckily, Neil was close enough to the ledge to slide down the last few metres on his bottom. We threw up our tents on the first flat spot we could find and, with daybreak only a few hours away, we decided to wait until then to make a move again. We were camped on a mountainside where the ground rolled steeply and threateningly down to the valley below.

The pouring rain reminded me of a race in the Lake District when I'd taken shelter in a public convenience after finding my sleeping bag was wet through. Sitting on the toilet seat, I fell forward until my chest rested on my trousers, and the back of my hands dropped down to rest on the top of my feet. I hung my head down over my knees. Amazingly, the position was relaxing, soothing and warm, and I slept for a full hour.

I had no such luxury now; the only positive was that daylight was not too far away to help us on our journey. We had navigated about 150 metres too far to the right, and instead of following the valley floor, we had continued to contour the mountainside. We were trudging along a perilous cliff edge amongst the dense forest sprawled over the mountain terrain for miles. Our going was slower than ever as the density of the forest thickened. We were climbing, scrambling and falling. Fred's feet gave him diabolical pain, and Thomas and Neil were virtually silent.

Another night crept up on us, and after our cliff-edge experience the previous night, we decided to set up camp and stay put during the darkest hours, from midnight until approximately 4 a.m. The last few hours of the trek seemed to take forever. We stumbled into the next checkpoint tent, talking very little but eating ravenously. I ate an entire pack of Pringles, then wished I hadn't.

Thomas and I left the tent and began assembling our bikes for the next stage. The organisers quickly warned us that we only had one hour to cycle the remaining 45 kilometres. It was apparent we were not going to make it. Our race was over.

I returned from Patagonia disappointed we had not finished but pleased I had survived a tough expedition. We had a good team, but the Last Wild Race was true to its name – wilder than I could have imagined.

Back home, a surprise was waiting for me. Three other cyclists planned to cycle to the South Pole in the Antarctic summer of 2013, the same time I was planning my expedition. I was now facing competition from an Australian, an American and a Spaniard.

# 10. Icelandic Glacier Training

"Doubting yourself is the first step to failure"

With only a few months to go, it was time for the final and most important decision of all—could I afford to realise my dream? I had no title sponsor and was still unsure whether the Polar Cycle was equipped for the job.

My estimated costs for the expedition were a frightening £120,000, and the only way to meet it was to use every penny of my savings and take some loans. This would saddle me with the burden of a 25-year repayment term. Unlike a mortgage, I could potentially have nothing at the end of it if I were to fail. Even if I did succeed, there would be no guarantee of financial reward. I felt very nervous.

If I wasn't going to gain sponsorship successfully before the expedition, then I needed a way of making money afterwards. With ITV on board and guaranteed television coverage, I needed to ensure I captured excellent footage and didn't want to rely only on myself for this. I needed to focus on cycling. Our agreement was that ITV would make the programme and air it once, and I would then have full rights to the programme for future sales. Wayne and my father battled over who should help me film my expedition and sit in a truck on the Antarctic ice for long, cold hours. Wayne had never had to live out in very cold temperatures before, but he was determined to support me. This convinced me that our regular fiery exchanges, which had been building to a crescendo during the year due to our wildly different commitments, were simply a show of care and concern. Wayne's decision to support me was also a great relief to my father.

Wayne and I were creatures of a similar mould, though some of our cultural differences sometimes continued to spark frenetic arguments. We were both driven by some innate desire to be the best we could at what we did. Fortunately, Wayne's aims were deeply embedded in the business world, whereas mine were spread across business and adventure sports. Despite many differences in outlook, we were committed to supporting each other in our different exploits.

As Wayne was now going to accompany me on my expedition, I had to consider him also. To help acclimatise him and to test my Polar Cycle in Antarctic conditions, we decided on a short trip to Iceland. Wayne had never been in temperatures anywhere near what we would be experiencing, and I was very nervous about the outcome. I focused the next few days on ensuring Wayne had all the kit he needed to keep warm. The head office of Arctic Trucks, which was helping me with transport in Antarctica, was based in Iceland, so our trip doubled up as a good chance to meet the team and confirm the logistics.

When we landed in Reykjavik, Gudmundor from Arctic Trucks met us. He had been my main point of contact in negotiating costs for overland vehicle travel for the expedition. He turned up at our youth hostel with a very brash Toyota Hilux, which had been converted by Arctic Trucks into a snow and ice-devouring machine. Its 44-inch tyres required a leg up to get into, and I understood completely why the Top Gear team had immediately latched onto these vehicles for their North Pole mission. Not only did it make you look like the coolest kid in town, but the float with the enormous wheels was incredible.

It was snowing lightly, and the temperature was below zero as we arrived at the Arctic Trucks headquarters, about 30 minutes outside Reykjavik. I planned a brief visit to discuss logistics with Emil before heading out to the Langjökull glacier, the second largest in Iceland, to test the Polar Cycle. Emil appeared at the entrance as we arrived and having become acquainted with him over Skype during the past year, I felt a great relief to meet him finally. He was softly spoken with a welcoming, caring attitude, contradictory to his rugged appearance. He was due to leave for Antarctica the next day to begin his expedition with Walking with the Wounded, so our timing had been spot on. Meeting him in the flesh began to turn my expedition into reality. I was surrounded by people who were a fundamental lifeline to this mission. I was bubbling with excitement and couldn't wait to hear his opinion on the Polar Cycle that we had nurtured and developed for the job. Until now, I had kept it a secret from almost everyone, Emil included.

I felt tense because I knew the reactions and opinions of Emil, Gudmundor, Gisli, and other Arctic Truck employees would be fundamental to my morale as they all had vast experience of polar travel. Wayne and I unpacked the massive cardboard box we had taped up sturdily in the UK for its flight to Iceland. The Arctic Truck team watched keenly as we assembled the Polar Cycle, section by section. I gazed up at their faces to gauge their initial reaction, and I could see Emil's eyes light up and a gentle smile creep across the left side of his mouth. I felt like a kid in a playground waiting for approval of my brand-new toy.

As the unpacking progressed, the third wheel and the recumbent seat received approval from the Icelanders. We put the frame together "Do you think it will work?" I asked.

"Wheels have proved a great success in Antarctic snow conditions, with stability being the key. Three wheels is a great idea," said Emil. I sat back on the recumbent seat to demonstrate the relaxed position I would be cycling in, and the guys gave me a nod of approval. This filled me with delight.

It was now time to talk business, so Wayne, Emil, Gudmundor and I headed up to the boardroom on the first floor to talk through the logistics. I felt a sense of calm as we walked through the office, shaking hands with the friendly members of the staff.

As a skier was planning to ski from the Ross Ice Shelf to the South Pole around the time of my expedition, we discussed how we could share logistics and transport costs to save money. We would meet the trucks at the South Pole and then be driven to our start point, almost 700 kilometres away, where we would be dropped off to begin our long journey back to the Pole.

The door opened hastily behind me before we'd even sat down around the boardroom table. Gudmundor announced quietly and abruptly that our expedition was in jeopardy. The skier had decided to pull out of his expedition. This left me with an unexpected dilemma. To conform to minimum safety standards in Antarctica, two vehicles are mandatory; should one fall down a crevasse, then the winching system of the other would hopefully pull the fallen vehicle to safety. Now, I had two trucks to pay for instead of one.

With a barrel of the most expensive fuel in the world costing over $5,000, a rate per kilometre plus the daily rate for the drivers was an incredible amount to add to my mounting bill. Our contract was for a twenty-day expedition, so to reduce costs, my only option was to finish the journey in half the time—a goal I aspired to but couldn't guarantee.

We discussed the plans repeatedly and tried to work out how to go ahead without any party losing out. Gudmundor reminded us that all expeditions needed to have bad weather days planned into the schedule, which added to the minefield of uncertainties. Will the Polar Cycle allow me to cover the distance required to complete the expedition in good time? What was the probability that I would make it to the top of the Leverett Glacier on the Polar Cycle without any problems? How much bad weather could I sustain before having to sit it out in my tent? Frustratingly, the questions were unanswerable.

The Icelandic nature is one of honesty, trust, and sticking to one's word. Finally, we reached an agreement on the contract. My expedition would go ahead. Nevertheless, I felt uneasy, and my earlier calmness was replaced with apprehension. There was so much pressure on me to make this happen in a shorter time than I had planned. I simply could not fail all the people and goodwill now involved in the expedition. My breathing shortened as I headed to the bathroom. Tears rolled down my face, and my chest was heaving as my breathing became erratic and I broke into sweat. I learnt a vital lesson as I sat on the toilet seat with my face in my hands. I must not doubt myself but control my feelings and proceed with a sense of numbness to gain the strength to complete what I had come here to do. I had to be strong and focus on my next few days on the glacier. The time had come to put the Polar Cycle to the test.

We departed from Emil's office for the Langjökull Glacier, embarking on a four-hour drive into the Icelandic wilds in a modified truck. There were no houses or animals in sight. It was just after 3 pm, and dusk was starting to fall. Leaving behind Reykjavik, the route became hilly and barren. After a few hours, we turned off the main road and bumped along a track. It became steeper and rougher by the minute. The snow thickened into large, blinding snowflakes that swarmed out of the darkness. Joi, our driver and mechanic, seemed unphased by the fact that there was no road to follow. It was blowing a gale, and visibility was down to zero. His GPS was his only guide.

We received a radio call from another team that was out training on the glacier and planning to ski in Antarctica during the same season as I was. They were already at the foot of the glacier, but their vehicle, a six-wheeler with an extra-long wheelbase, was struggling to climb it. "We'll be there soon to help them," said Joi calmly. We caught up with the truck in difficulty, and after some brief instructions to the driver, Joi had both trucks crawling up the glacier. This final section of the journey to the top took three hours.

The temperature outside was a nippy minus 15 degrees Celsius, and a complete whiteout surrounded us, so all we could do was stare earnestly at the GPS. Silent, chunky snowflakes blanketed the windscreen. It was hard to comprehend that I would be out in these conditions in the next few hours, on my own, on my Polar Cycle. I was keen to compare Iceland's Langjökull Glacier with the Leverett Glacier, which I would be climbing in Antarctica. Emil had told me that the first section of the glacier was approximately ten kilometres and resembled the steepness of the moderate parts of the Leverett Glacier but not its very steep sections. Due to the complete whiteout and lack of visibility, I was none the wiser about the conditions I would face under my tyres.

The wind and snow were blowing a gale as we arrived at our camp for the weekend. Stephan, the guide for the other group on the glacier and who knew the area well, told us to build a snow wall about three feet deep to protect the tents from the prevailing wind. The snow on the glacier was light and fluffy, like candy floss, so each scoop blew off the shovel as we battled against the wind. All I could think about was whether the Polar Cycle would cope with the conditions.

With a poorly built snow wall for protection, we decided it was time to fight with the tent's canvas and erect it as fast as possible. Blinded by the snow and hardly able to stand up, the canvas flapped viciously as we strove to erect the tent. We had to pin it down securely with ice screws and walls of snow piled up on the material valances around the base of the tent. Wayne was doing exceedingly well despite landing in the worst conditions of his life. We crawled into the tent as Stephan hastily threw us some freeze-dried bags of food as a consolation prize. "These are some of the worst conditions I've seen on this glacier," he commented. We fired up our stove and heated our freeze-dried food solemnly. The wind was howling, and the tent flaps whistled in an inharmonious symphony. I was worried the Polar Cycle would disappear in the blizzard.

Time was limited, so I took the Polar Cycle for its first real test. I didn't want to wait until morning despite night-time rapidly creeping up on me. Wrapped up snugly in my down jacket and carrying my head torch and GPS, Joi helped me lift my Polar Cycle off the back of the truck. I explained my plan to cycle down the glacier on the route we'd just driven up for about three kilometres and then turn around and cycle straight back up. I left instructions that he would come and find me if he didn't see me within the next three hours. I noted that Joi had been reducing the air pressure in the vehicle tyres on our drive up, so

I followed his example and reduced the pressure in my three tyres to 3psi. This would cause a lot more drag, but hopefully, I would gain traction. I discussed the optimum psi for the conditions with Joi. It was an important detail that I needed to master, and Joi was the man with the knowledge.

It was one in the morning, and I was faced with the worst possible conditions for training. Yet paradoxically, it was a perfect test. I was excited as I began to pedal off into the darkness. I had barely left the camp when my chain snapped. Joi must have been watching me because he hurried over to see why my head torch was flickering back and forth rather than gradually disappearing in the distance. I hoped he didn't think I was rude when I demanded to be left alone. In Antarctica, I would have to deal with such problems alone as I was planning an unsupported expedition.

I reached into my pannier bag to pull out my chain tool and tried to fix the chain. Attempt after attempt failed as the wind blew the chain and my gloved hands uncontrollably, and I was left with little dexterity. I was cold and tired, and suddenly, my disturbed sleep over the last two months accumulated into a feeling of total distress. The five-second limit that I could take my hands out of my gloves was not long enough to fix the chain—twenty minutes passed. I was now shivering violently and swearing incessantly.

The simple job of fixing a chain had become impossible in the conditions. I ran through the process in my mind and decided that my next attempt would work. I removed my outer glove, sheltered my hands with my back turned to the wind, opened my eyes wide into the beam of my head torch and focused my brain. "I can do this," I told myself. Miraculously, my determination worked. I sorted the chain out, brushed off the mound of accumulated snow on my seat and was back on board, freezing and desperate to get going. I could feel the cold penetrate straight through my trousers and deep into my butt cheeks. The snow was soft, and the going was frustratingly tough. I began to pant. To add to my misery, I constantly used my hands on the tyres to create the traction I needed. I felt demoralised and began to realise how much my success in Antarctica depended on firm snow conditions.

Back in the Arctic Trucks office, Gisli had seemed confident that the conditions in Antarctica were better for wheels than the glaciers in Iceland. I hung this advice on a reassuring string around my neck that I could call upon during moments of doubt. I had covered only about two kilometres down the glacier when I decided to turn around and head back to camp. The pedalling was tougher, and now, with only light snow covering pure ice, I realised that studs in the rear tyres were essential. I'd added a few back at the Arctic Trucks headquarters but double the amount would be needed to tackle the exposed ice in Antarctica.

I made it back to camp, tied the Polar Cycle to our tent and collapsed inside with a mixture of sheer exhaustion and frustration. For the hundredth time, I began to doubt my expedition to Antarctica. It was early morning, and the wind was ferocious. I felt guilty for putting Wayne through this discomfort. He was lying covered in layers of down sleeping bags, but I could tell he was not getting any sleep. The noise from the wind drowned any conversation, so we waited silently for the sun to rise.

As dawn broke, I was up again to tackle more testing. Visibility was minimal, and the snow was soft and fluffy. I made little progress, travelling only a matter of metres before jumping up from my seat and attempting to kick and push the Polar Cycle over the next large mound of snow. This was never going to work.

Noticeably upset, Joi came over to me and suggested that they made some tracks with the trucks around the top of the glacier that I could follow. This provided enough space for two wheels to travel in the tracks. I bit my lip and scolded myself for succumbing to his support, but it did make a difference. Travelling down the glacier was exhilarating, but a fundamental lack of braking power developed as my speed picked up. I skidded from left to right as the tyre tracks from the vehicle caused the Polar Cycle to veer uncontrollably.

I managed to regain some control by directing the Polar Cycle out of the tracks at a slight angle to the glacier. However, this compromised my stability, forcing me to hang desperately over my left wheel. Fortunately, I managed to keep all wheels on the ground as I came to a stop. I'd packed my quick-release harness into my panniers that morning because I realised that if I had no luck cycling up the Leverett Glacier, which for me would be a worst-case scenario, then at least I could tow the Polar Cycle and I needed the practice. Cycling uphill was a no-go due to the ice and lack of studs in my tyres, so I began to tow the Polar Cycle. The weight with all my kit was unbearable, and I struggled to maintain my footing as each step slipped away from underneath me.

I also needed studs in my Polar boots. Without them, I couldn't cycle or tow. It couldn't get any worse.

Joi appeared further up the glacier and asked if I wanted a hand. He tossed me a rope and told me to hold on. For the next eight kilometres,

I was dragged by his vehicle up the glacier. It was a total disaster, and I was on the verge of breaking down that evening.

Nothing worked. All the pressures that came with an expedition of this scale descended on me like a ton of bricks. I was nearing my end and so upset that I missed the once-in-a-lifetime opportunity of seeing the Northern Lights blazing across the sky. I was sitting in my tent feeling desperate when Stefan appeared and reassured me that conditions like this, with soft and slippery snow, were unlikely in Antarctica because there was far less moisture in the air. Gisli also told me that the snow conditions in Antarctica were unique. Though classed as a desert with a covering of snow, the extreme cold and lack of moisture meant that the snow tended to firm quickly, and piles of sastrugi became rock solid in minutes. I prayed this would provide better going.

On our final morning on the glacier, I witnessed the most beautiful sunrise, seemingly giving me hope. The weather was calm, and the skies were blue. The temperature had dropped dramatically overnight, the wind had ceased to blow, and the snow was beginning to compact. There was a glimmer of hope for my last trial. Without breakfast or a second thought, I crawled out of the tent before Wayne stirred and headed off down the other side of the glacier. The conditions had changed significantly, and the Polar Cycle glided above the snow sufficiently for me to turn the pedals without compromising traction.

I headed out of our camp for about ten kilometres to the middle of the glacier, and after a few hours, Joi and Wayne appeared in the truck to check my progress. It was the first time I had a smile since arriving on the glacier. After a few more hours of cycling, I realised that with a firmer crust of snow over the surface, the Polar Cycle might just work. It was aerodynamic, comfortable and could carry up to 90 kilograms of kit. I returned to our camp to help pack up, feeling far more positive.

We had planned some crevasse rescue training before leaving, so Stefan drove us to an area of the glacier with plenty of crevasses to practice falling in and hauling each other out. I hadn't ice climbed for many years, and it was fun to be back in a pair of crampons with ice axes in my hands. We spent half a day climbing in and out of a small crevasse about 15 metres deep. It was essential that Wayne could learn and understand the techniques as well, and being highly practical, he picked it up quickly. Crevasse training is not compulsory but highly recommended for anyone setting foot in Antarctica.

The training reminded me of the many weekends I spent ice climbing some winter routes in the Scottish hills. On one occasion, I even tackled the classic Point Five Gully on the north face of Ben Nevis. The five-pitch climb took my boyfriend Will and I twelve hours to reach the top, where there was a huge overhanging ice cornice that we had to hack a hole through to climb to the summit. It was a very exposed route with reducing visibility that I climbed with him back in 2005, with no water, no compass, just a hip flask of whisky. We had driven up from Portsmouth with a mission to climb Ben Nevis, but we were young and inexperienced and needed a real concept of risk. It was the biggest, most dangerous winter climb I had ever tackled, hammering ice screws into blocks of ice, putting both our lives at risk with little respect for safety.

# 11. The Land I Dreamt Of

*"When you have everything to lose,*
*stay focused and believe in yourself"*

With only three days to go until our flight from Heathrow to Cape Town, which I had already booked, I still needed a sponsor to cover the astronomical cost of the expedition. Everything was in the balance. Perching on the edge of our bed in our apartment, reality hit. I had no savings left as all had been absorbed by the spending so far.

"It's over!" I cried with frustration, looking up towards Wayne, who was standing in the doorway to the bedroom. "I've got no sponsor because no one believes in me. I've tried to be strong and focused, but I'm at my end. I can't do this anymore," I screamed as my shoulders shook uncontrollably.

Wayne joined me on the bed and sat with his arms tightly around me. "You can't give up now; there is a way." I was crying so hard I hadn't really heard what he said. "You've put so much into this; you can't give up now", he continued.

I'd researched possible loans I'd had partially approved, but now the time had come to act, and I didn't have the strength to do so. I was doubting my own ability to succeed. "I can't believe I've wasted four years of my life and yours," I spluttered.

"Look," Wayne said, shaking my shoulders and partially interrupting my almost incomprehensible sentences, "I'm happy to lend you the money," he said.

He knew how important the expedition was to me, but panic hit me when I realised I'd be indebted to him for the rest of my life. What if I couldn't pay him back? And how would this now affect the dynamics of our relationship? "I can't accept that," I said, still in tears. I was shaking all over, my face was bright red, tears soaked into my top, and I was back in my dark place. It was the worst place ever, and I'd promised myself it would never happen again. It had been four years since my episode of depression, and for the first time, I felt I was close to revisiting it. "This isn't how it's meant to be. I need a sponsor; I need someone to say yes, this is an incredible thing you're about to do, and we definitely want to be part of it," I screamed. But I was creating only a fairy-tale world of how I wished it should be.

"I believe in you," Wayne said in a calm voice.

"Of course, you should," I said abruptly, "you're my boyfriend." On the verge of offending him, I left the flat, still crying. I needed air, and I needed space.

Standing in the lift, I realised I'd not thanked him for his offer, nor had I even acknowledged it. Everything was exploding right in front of me, and I was falling apart. I now had a lot of parties who had invested time and effort in my expedition, and the one straw to success that Wayne had just offered me, I had almost thrown straight back into his face. What was I doing, and why did I consider this offer an offence? To me, not securing the sponsorship I needed was a complete failure on my part. I walked around Cardiff Bay angry with myself, oblivious of anyone else or where I was going. I was in a different world.

"Where have you been?" Wayne said on my return. "I'm sorry," I said, "I'm just so upset that I haven't managed to get the sponsorship, and the last thing I want to do is gamble with your hard-earned money," I continued.

"The offer is still there, so just let me know," he said in a calm, reassuring voice. I felt so fortunate, but at the same time, I was now utterly petrified of what could be. Would he now own me? Would this now be his expedition? I felt trapped, but I had no other option if I wanted this to go ahead.

"What if I never manage to pay you back," I continued negatively.

"We'll deal with that later. Right now, you've got to focus on getting this world record," he said. I hated the idea that Wayne would now have every right to influence my expedition. This was my thing, and I needed to do it my way if I was to succeed. Still, with tears rolling down my cheeks and eyes swollen and puffy, we sat for an uncomfortable silence on the sofa, looking out on the water where sailing boats were cruising back and forth. "I can't ask you to pay for the expedition; it's just too much," I said during a break in my self-pity.

That was, in fact, my bizarre way of saying, "Yes, I'll take the money." I was completely unable to accept his kind offer directly. I needed Wayne to decide for me. All I now needed him to say was, "Okay, so that's settled. I fund it." Instead, Wayne sighed and said, "It's up to you." A little person inside me was kicking me like mad, telling me to 'woman up' and accept the offer, but my pride would not allow me to voice this view.

We went to bed that night with no further discussion, and the following morning, I didn't get up for my training programme for the first time in over a year. Right now, fitness was not important.

"As long as you're sure, Wayne, then yes, I'd like to take you up on your offer to fund the expedition," I said in a shaky voice over breakfast. He leaned over to me and said, "I'm so pleased. You've put so much into this, and I want you to succeed."

Sitting alongside Wayne as he made three large transfers to cover the cost of the expedition, I was truly committed, and my fear of failure was at an all-time high. The reality of a lifetime financial commitment was hard to swallow, coupled with the pressure of trying to complete the expedition in record time to save costs—but I had no option. I had come this far, and I was not turning back.

I spent some time during the final month trying to glean as much information as possible on the other two cyclists. Fortunately, they'd been posting all over the internet for the last six months about their plans, whereas I'd kept everything secret. The third cyclist had already deferred her attempt to the following year. My two competitors were starting from Hercules Inlet, and neither appeared very experienced in polar conditions. The Spaniard seemed more experienced than the American, but both had poor plans. They were going to be towing sledges. The American was planning to go supported and the Spaniard unsupported. The Spaniard had skis with him and the ability to tow his bike on his sledge. They had both chosen the longer but far less steep route to the Pole.

I was quietly confident of my plan, but the unknown was still huge, and I couldn't take anything for granted. The one issue that made me panic was that they were setting off in two days at the end of November, whereas I had to wait until December 17 to begin my traverse. They would have a three-week head start. During the last few weeks, I was constantly tense and a little irritable, and though Wayne was excited about my unique expedition, he feared for my safety. The plan was for Wayne to join Emil and Torfi, who would drive the vehicles that would transport me to my start line on the Ross Ice Shelf at the base of the Transantarctic Mountain Range. As I was planning an unsupported expedition, all they could do was follow from a distance, take the occasional photograph and capture some video footage at key moments.

I sat in the middle of the sitting room floor, trying to reduce the pile of kit that lay around me, constantly balancing weight with need. I reduced my sock pile to two pairs. As knickers had two sides and I could turn them over, two pairs would suffice. I decided against packing thick down trousers and took a lighter pair for ease of movement, but I took my thick down jacket, some wrags, which are headscarves that double up as kidney warmers and knee protection and, most important of all, my polar boots that I had been stomping around in for weeks, sweating profusely.

Wayne tried to make useful suggestions but always found himself in trouble as I intermittently snapped at him for no good reason. I wanted his help but wouldn't allow myself to listen to him. I had to be confident in my decisions, and I could only do this by making them myself, based on my previous experience in cold temperatures.

Initially, my spares kit contained extra-large Allen keys with a T bar handle that would be easy to manoeuvre with thick gloves, but I decided to select just two for the most common adjustments, together with a combination tool with all sizes for the rest. Hopefully, they would not be needed, as trying to unscrew a bolt wearing three layers of gloves using a small combination tool was almost impossible. Should I take spare inner tubes and a tyre? I decided on two inner tubes, no tyre, one set of extra strong chains, and four bungees to attach my kit to the Polar Cycle frame. I piled gaffer tape around every part of the Polar Cycle as this was my solution for anything I would struggle to fix. I learnt from previous expeditions that gaffer tape can work miracles in the most difficult situations.

I needed water bottles, but as the contents would freeze immediately, this was going to be a big problem. On Lake Baikal, keeping my INOV8 hydration system against my body worked well, provided I remembered to blow air back into the tube after each sip to retain all water well inside the bladder of the hydration system and not in the tube where it would freeze. My body acted as a great heater. I also took a thermos flask wrapped with an extra coating of Thinsulate material. I wondered if this would be sufficient protection at minus 40 degrees Celsius.

I was fastidious about stripping down the Polar Cycle during my packing session, so I knew how it was all put together by heart. I'd been back to Inspired Cycle Engineering's warehouse, where Chris, the technical director, had taken me through the finer details of the Polar Cycle. I was finally confident I could rebuild it should it fall apart on the ice. In reality, I knew that rebuilding the Polar Cycle in Antarctica would be impossible without freezing to death first.

"Maria, you need a break. Do you want a cup of tea?" Wayne intervened. I was trying to replace the extremely long chain on my Polar Cycle. The three tyres were strewn across the floor, and the Polar Cycle was balancing upside down in an unstable position on an old cardboard box. I was trying to replace the chain with my gloves on, struggling to locate the bottom bracket at the same time as the Polar Cycle began rocking on the box. "No!" I said sharply. "Can't you see I'm in the middle of something, and I'm timing myself. Leave me alone."

By now, Wayne knew how to deal with me. We'd explode into an argument in the past, but now he turned around and left the room. I tried to attach the chain three times more before admitting he was right once again. It was 4 pm, and I'd not had any lunch. It was time for a break.

Pulling up the bookmarked pages showing the other two cyclists' blogs, I could breathe more easily as I saw their daily struggle. The Spaniard was ahead and making better progress than the American. Still, his progress was very slow, and it seemed he was doing more skiing and towing his bike rather than cycling, so could it be classed as a cycling expedition?

Over the remaining days before departure, I packed and repacked my panniers. I created Excel sheets which detailed exactly what items were in each pannier on the Polar Cycle, including their position. Was it on the right or left, and if so, was it in the front or back? I needed to be confident that I could retrieve what I was looking for the first time around. I had six panniers and had to ensure that my weight distribution was even. Food made up most of the weight, so this was distributed equally across all six bags. The remaining space in three panniers was split between clothes, Polar Cycle spares, and first aid. I rested my tent and sleeping bag on the top of the Polar Cycle frame so they were instantly accessible and would double up as a headrest.

I needed a break from my pre-expedition frenzy, so my second trip to the fitness training facility at Loughborough University, just two weeks before departure, was timely. I wanted to know if all my training had paid off. I was accompanied by ITV Wales, who liked to capture my expressions of pain for the documentary during a second day of strenuous physical testing—the only comfort being that it would hopefully help pay back some of the loan through the sale of the documentary.

The experience was far from a training break. After fasting for over 12 hours, followed by a tough day of physical testing, I left exhausted and hungry. My results showed that my body's ability to burn fat had vastly improved, meaning I should be able to sustain the progress needed on minimal food intake. This was excellent news under emergency survival circumstances. On the other hand, there was a problem with my cardiovascular ability. I had a very definitive maximum breathing level, which, for some reason, I couldn't improve. My legs were super strong, but my breathing capacity let me down. This meant that with high-intensity exercise, I was unlikely to be able to push as hard as someone else of equal fitness.

It wasn't until a couple of years later, when I visited a private medical facility in London that I was diagnosed with asthma. Despite having strong lungs, I only used about 60% of them. This was a shock to me as I assumed that my brief encounter with asthma as a young child had passed and it was normal to feel like I did when I pushed myself to the maximum: gasping for breath, feeling dizzy with a tight wheezing chest and with limited ability to extract the air from my lungs. If only I'd known earlier, I would have used asthma medication and saved myself much discomfort. Having said that, would I even have contemplated a world-first expedition?

I downplayed the importance of my cardiovascular fitness, telling myself that the expedition relied more on survival skills, endurance, and intelligence than on optimal physical condition. Confident in my body's fat-burning efficiency and the mental strength I gained from consistent positive visualisation, I felt prepared to tackle the last week of preparations. Facing obstacles only fuelled my enthusiasm, as I thrived on overcoming challenges.

My head was buzzing with questions. Will I be able to pay back my debts? Will my potentially severe knee injury be a showstopper? Will Wayne still want to be with me after all this? What would it feel like to freeze to death? What if my chosen route is not the right one, and one of the other cyclists claims the title? Do I have enough clothes with me? Do I have enough food and fuel? Does Wayne still love me? That damn Leverett Glacier! Can I honestly climb it and reach the South Pole in record time?

Interspersed with my doubts, I consoled myself with the thought:

'I'm the luckiest person on Earth to have this opportunity. I've worked hard to make it happen, and I'm so, so, so excited I can barely think!' The atmosphere was buzzing with a mixture of emotions as I hugged my parents goodbye at Heathrow Airport; we were finally on our way. I was going to Antarctica to claim a world-first title. What could be better? Despite my thorough packing practice, all kit and equipment ended up in two large cardboard boxes, heavily gaffer taped and identifiable, with my contact details written in permanent pen all over them. Unexpectedly, I had to open it all up again at the airport and re-distribute it into four cardboard boxes instead of two to conform to airline regulations. I had made my first mistake by not checking the rules. What if one box got lost during transit? I could end up with only three-quarters of a Polar Cycle. Fortunately, I could not dwell on these fears as we had only 13 minutes to run to the departure gate. We were about to miss the first part of our very long journey. Wayne passed no comment, but I could feel his thoughts; I had been very careless.

After flying into Cape Town, we spent three frustrating days dealing with constantly changing flight dates for our onward flight to Antarctica. The uncertainty was exasperating, and I was desperate to move on, especially as there was only one onward flight. Flying into Antarctica was only the beginning of my journey; I would have to endure up to a week of travel across the continent just to arrive at the start point.

During my stay in Cape Town, I consumed a massive amount of food, and the last evening was no exception. For the first time in my life, I ordered so much food that I couldn't finish my meal. Even though I had done no exercise for almost five days, I didn't seem to be putting on weight, so I assumed I was burning off the excess nervous energy. I started to feel concerned about maintaining the fitness I had worked so hard to build up to my genetic maximum.

Once again, I used the waiting time to assemble and dismantle the cycle to ensure I had a picture in my mind of every inch of the cycle and the contents of my panniers. I was so well prepared that there was absolutely nothing left to do. Nothing at all.

The last day in Cape Town seemed endless. I spent most of it at the ALCI office and the shopping mall, eating yet more food and buying some biltong to supplement my snack bags. Biltong was a food I would never eat at home, but it would be a different story in Antarctica. The look of it repulsed me, but after plenty of persuasion from Wayne, a biltong lover, I knew that its high protein content would help keep me going on my expedition.

Finally, at 10 am on December 11, I had confirmation from Anne at the ALCI office that a flight would be leaving that evening. I was ready and waiting, and after the last traumatic episode repacking my cycle at Heathrow, this time, I could fly with the Polar Cycle assembled.

The flight was due to leave at 11.30 pm, and on arrival at the airport, I was thrilled to see the flight board display 'Antarctica, 11:30 pm, Gate 11.' It seemed unbelievable that I was en route to catch that very plane. Unlike regular check-in desks, my check-in consisted of chatting with three Russian men standing in the departure lounge, who casually handed me my ticket and fast-tracked me through security, saying, "Let her through. She's going to Antarctica." I felt like royalty! On the plane were some people who worked for the ALCI airbase, a group from the adventure company White Desert and a couple flying to Antarctica to get married!

As I approached the plane, all standard airport and aircraft etiquette seemed to disappear, and I walked freely around the plane before boarding. It was an Ilyushin Il-76TD Russian-designed heavy cargo transporter. At first sight, it looked like a fighter jet with its sharply pointed nose covered in glass. As I climbed up the very steep, rickety ladder into the body of the aircraft, I was amazed at what I saw. There was no interior cladding, and the internal frame of the fuselage, with all its pipes, nuts, bolts and cables hanging down, looked as though it was only partially finished. I wondered whether this plane was ready to fly or was still in its build stage.

There were five rows of seats, and the remainder of the plane was full of cargo stacked haphazardly in the aircraft's main cabin. Much to my surprise, the facilities consisted of two portaloos strapped firmly into place and just behind them was a 4x4 truck, plenty of fuel barrels and my Polar Cycle. It was all somewhat incongruous. The air host was a Russian male, plain-clothed officer who looked about twelve years old and seemed very at home handing out endless sandwiches and chocolate bars. As I took my seat, I checked out the oxygen masks that were scattered all over the plane. I wondered what altitude we would be flying at and decided to check out the masks so I knew how they operated. All aboard, we began to taxi to the runway. The thundering noise inside the aircraft was deafening, and even with earplugs, I felt like I was sitting in an engine testing facility. At the front of the plane was a huge screen mirroring the cockpit, from which I could see the whole take-off. The journey lasted for six and a half hours, and instead of resting, I remained obsessed with how strange everything felt.

Shortly before landing, a large notice appeared on the screen saying,

"We will be landing in Antarctica in about forty minutes; please change into your Antarctic clothing." I leapt into action and pulled out all my Mountain Equipment clothing and Baffin polar boots, which, according to the manufacturers, were rated to keep my feet warm up to minus 100 degrees Celsius. As a result, for the remaining part of the flight, I sat melting in my Polar gear.

The runway at Novolazarevskaya was a blue ice runway, and the Russian pilot landed the massive Illuysian seamlessly onto the ice. I barely felt the plane touchdown. I was now in the endless whiteness of Antarctica, and from that first moment of contact, my love for this elusive continent began to flow.

Antarctica had been out of reach for so many years, and my dream was finally becoming a reality. I felt like a child bubbling with excitement. Paradoxically, Wayne, who was understandably apprehensive about what he'd let himself in for, now realised there was no turning back. I was delighted that he was with me, and I knew he was here for my safety, but at the same time, it created extra pressure and tension because I was concerned about how he was feeling.

The aircraft door opened, and a ladder was erected against the exit door. We were reminded about the risk of slipping when stepping off the ladder. Following my slippery experience on the glacier in Iceland, I had small studs in my boots, so I knew I wouldn't have a problem leaping off the second but last step so I could dance around with excitement. I was finally standing on Antarctic ice.

I loved the cold, but this felt exceptionally cold. I pictured myself in a tent and imagined I might freeze to death despite my previous cold weather experience. I tried to banish the thought from my mind. A few other passengers were promptly collected by trucks and driven off, and Wayne and I were left standing on the runway with one or two other stragglers. We hung around to watch the cargo being unloaded as I wanted to ensure that the Polar Cycle made it off safely. The cold soon began to seep through my clothing, and I gazed at Wayne constantly to assess how he was thinking and feeling. We had spoken only briefly on the plane because of the noise, and I began to feel guilty about putting him through such an ordeal. From the outset, he looked totally calm and already adjusted to the environment, but I wondered how long this would last.

Before the intense cold could affect us, a Russian named Boris arrived in his truck. He invited us to hop in for a tour. With a few days to spare before a suitable weather window for my next flight, I was eager to discover the airbase and its surroundings.

Novolazarevskaya is located at Dronning Maud Land in the eastern part of Antarctica. The area was discovered by Norwegian explorers in 1929 and named after Queen Maud of Norway. Rather than being divided east to west by the South Pole, Antarctica is bisected by the Transantarctic Mountains. Most of the continent is situated east of this mountain range. To get to the start point of my expedition, I would have to fly east from Novolazarevskaya to the South Pole, catch a lift with the Arctic Truck convoy to the Ross Ice Shelf and, once at the edge of the continent, begin my cycle east again to the South Pole.

At first sight, the airbase looked like it had been dropped out of the sky. About fifteen shipping containers sitting on huge metal ski bases lay randomly on the ice. I had seen pictures from the Walking with the Wounded expedition and, therefore, had some idea of what to expect. Although I had prepared myself for camping, I was lucky to be allocated a bed in one of the containers. The container even had a bathroom, but unfortunately, the only convenience was a urinal, so I had to learn quickly how to pee with precision standing up. The sitting down option meant a trip to another container, and coupled with the necessary clothing routine, it was an alternative I did not relish.

I dedicated the waiting time to Polar Cycle improvements, testing it time and time again and applying more thread locker to the screws. I ate everything I could get my hands on and became very fond of the mealtime routine. Breakfast was served at 8 am. At 7:58 am, groups of scientists would materialise as if out of thin air and sequentially make their way into the dining container. As they entered, they would shed their glasses, hats, coats, and gloves, revealing lengthy beards and hair that the harsh Antarctic environment had styled wonderfully.

They were a combination of Russian, Argentinean, and German scientists and pilots from Canada. The chefs cooked up a treat of Russian delights every day, and my first lunch at the airbase comprised beef and beetroot soup, which brought back memories of my time in Siberia.

Just outside the canteen container, I came across the only bird I had observed throughout my time in Antarctica. This solitary, robust bird with brown and white plumage, a Skua, sat peacefully on the ice. Likely having been carried astray by the wind, it had adapted to survive by befriending the airbase personnel, lining up for leftover food during mealtimes.

Only one woman was working on the airbase. She was the hostess who was responsible for checking visitors in and out. The problem was that she didn't speak much English, so sign language became our primary method of communication. She had a broad smile, which she used to replace conversation. I decided that I really should have learnt some Russian before this trip, but fortunately, Boris, the airbase manager, spoke good English and was easy to approach.

Porridge was my favourite breakfast choice, but the Russian style, richly layered with butter while providing an incredible number of calories, was difficult to digest, particularly as I'd filled my bowl to the brim. Breakfast lasted for half an hour, and everyone sat quietly to eat with minimum conversation. A bowl of chocolates was always available, and every mealtime, I grabbed a handful to complement the already highly calorific day bag that I would consume during my cycle. I continually feared that I would not have enough food and was always topping up my supplies like a compulsive squirrel. I adopted a charming Argentinean scientist as our friend, and we now sit next to him at mealtime. His English was far better than my Spanish. We talked mainly about how good the food was and whether it was a warm, cold day or a cold, cold day. I didn't know his name, and he didn't know mine. He didn't know what I was doing in Antarctica, and I assumed he was a scientist. We had the perfect mealtime relationship. After mealtimes, I took a nap, trying to bury my urgency to depart in sleep. Unfortunately, I still had to pee in the urinal.

A day later, a group of Americans arrived at the airbase in their converted Toyota Hilux vehicles, the same vehicles we had used in Iceland. They had just driven across Antarctica. They were filming their exploits for a US magazine and had to re-take their arrival with a rehearsed scene of congratulations. I stood nearby to try to overhear their conversation before I was brought into the group, and we exchanged hellos. As we shook hands, their gaze fell directly on my Polar Cycle, which I'd been tending to. "What's your plan?' asked the driver.

I felt awkward and nervous, and under my breath, I rattled out the words, "I'm going to cycle to the South Pole from the Ross Ice Shelf.

"We've just come from there," he said," It's a mega journey." Before I could launch into my one million desperate questions, they quickly remounted the vehicle and shot off into the distance. "Is mega a good thing or a bad thing," I pondered, annoyed that I had not managed to glean more information.

I heard later from Boris that they were staying in a guest house fifteen kilometres from the airbase. A guesthouse? I thought I was in the remotest part of the world. There was an ice road leading the whole way to the guest house, so I asked Boris to take me there to learn more about their experience. We pulled up at the guesthouse which lay in the middle of a vast area of rock. I wasn't sure if it was stunningly beautiful or reminded me of a scene from a James Bond film where the Russian scientists had a base in the middle of nowhere, from which helicopters would suddenly appear. It reminded me of pictures of the moon's surface and was the first time I had seen exposed rock in Antarctica. Outside the guest house stood the two Toyota Hilux vehicles with 44-inch wheels. As we entered the guesthouse, Russian etiquette ensued, and we were told to remove our shoes and replace them with some grandpa slippers. I chose a brown pair of really old man ones as I'd never had the pleasure of wearing such atrocious footwear. Scott, the owner of Overland magazine, Brett, the editor and their expedition team from the 7x7 challenge that involved driving across seven continents all sat around a table drinking coffee and eating biscuits.

"Hi," said Brett in a friendly American tone. "Do come in, and I'll show you some pictures from our journey." I chose a seat beside him, desperate to hear about the conditions. It turned out that they had just set the vehicle speed record for a traverse across Antarctica, and they had travelled my proposed route from the edge of the Ross Ice Shelf, up through the Transantarctic Mountain Range and onto the South Pole.

"This is a picture of the Leverett Glacier. It's pretty steep and a tough climb, but I think you'll be okay," continued Brett as I bent over his camera to view my destiny. From the pictures, it was difficult to understand the gradient, but the team were positive and encouraging, telling me they were sure I would make it and I should focus on the beauty of the mountains instead of worrying too much. After an hour and a half of chatting, we left, and Boris drove us back to the airbase. The images of this massive glacier were fresh in my mind, and I began pacing back and forth outside my cabin, continually checking through the Polar Cycle. "What if I just can't do it?"

I had twenty minutes to wait until lunchtime, so I lay on my bed, still in all my polar clothing. I'd packed and repacked my bags so many times that I couldn't think of anything else to do. After lunch with our Argentinean scientist friend who decided it was a hot, cold day today, I spent the rest of the day resting and sleeping whilst Wayne ensured he had enough coffee, biltong, steaks, whisky and DVDs packed securely to see him through a two to three-week residence in the truck.

Canadian pilot, Chuck declared at 5 pm that our flight was scheduled for 5 am the following day. I suddenly had so much to check out again with only twelve hours remaining. I needed to re-assemble the Polar Cycle, pack and re-pack a few more times, take more chocolate bars from the canteen and quietly endure waves of internal hysteria. My time had come. Since I'd spent most of the day sleeping, I did not rest that evening and spent most of the night chatting to a Turkish man who turned up at 11 pm. He was an engineer and had arrived at the airbase for a season of maintaining vehicles. I found out in the morning that he'd gone into the wrong bunk room, but I didn't mind; at least his chatter kept me occupied.

The chefs had laid on an early breakfast but I decided not to eat or drink anything as there would be no toilet on the plane and I was well aware that the cold temperature would make me want to wee more. A skidoo pulled up at my cabin to transport me to the plane, and I jumped on, piling my bags on the sledge behind. The Polar Cycle had been loaded the night before, and I was tingling with excitement about making another journey that would bring me a little bit closer to beginning my White Ice Cycle expedition.

The aircraft was a Basler Turbo, a modernised, turbine-powered version of the classic Douglas DC-3. In its blue, red and white livery, it looked super cool sitting on its skis in the middle of the expanse of whiteness. As I climbed on board, I was amazed to see the Polar Cycle strapped down next to the door, and further into the aircraft was a large engine. I hoped it was not the engine that was supposed to be flying the plane. I expected more passenger/cargo separation, but all are treated the same in the polar world. Chuck leapt on board and casually strutted up the gangway as though it was a catwalk. He was calm and relaxed. Was he capable of flying this plane?

Following closely behind was his co-pilot, sporting a cap on backwards, which looked somewhat out of place with his polar clothing. The air host in a fetching green all-in-one polar jumpsuit swiftly approached us as the only passengers on the plane and began briefing us. It didn't contain much, except if you'd like some oxygen, then ask. I fidgeted around to make myself comfortable and relaxed back in my seat, trying not to think of my bladder. Instead, I felt a headache starting to develop.

The eight-hour journey was in two parts. First, we flew to 83 degrees south to the most remote fuel station in the world. It consisted of a small tent and scattered barrels half buried in the snow that had been dropped from an aircraft. Here, two engineers spent two-month shifts ready to service the landing aircraft once or twice a week. Following a surveillance fly-by of the landing spot, Chuck lined up the Basler to land. Luckily, there was no taxiing involved, and the air host flung open the doors when we came to a stop. I leapt out of the plane and barely managed to make it to the back before my bladder exploded. As I hurriedly pulled up my trousers, my head began to throb more.

Here, we had a 12-hour compulsory stop for the pilot to rest so he could make the return journey with Prince Harry and the Walking with the Wounded team in one go. We erected tents in the endless snowy landscape, and I tried to sleep. However, my intense excitement only served to magnify the debilitating symptoms of altitude sickness. The swift ascent to high altitude, combined with the strain of immediate physical activity, the low atmospheric pressure, and the piercing cold of the arid environment, significantly escalated the symptoms. Now, at 2,600 metres, I felt sick with a blinding headache that relentlessly continued throughout the night and the remaining part of the flight.

# 12. No Turning Back

*"Thorough planning helps you prepare for the unplanned"*

As I disembarked from the plane at the South Pole, I could see figures approaching in the distance. When they came into view, I realised it was the Walking with the Wounded team. I was keen to shake hands with their leader, Ed Parker, whom I had only spoken to on the phone until now. He was a friendly and compassionate man, and throughout their journey to the Pole, he faced tough choices as the team encountered significantly harsher conditions than anticipated.

Prince Harry and Ed showed great interest when my Polar Cycle was lowered out of the aircraft, so I quickly hopped on to demonstrate what it could do. This turned out to be a terrible mistake. As I stood up after my enthusiastic demo, I found it difficult to stop my legs from shaking, and with the very real threat of vomiting on royalty due to a sudden wave of altitude sickness. As a result, my meeting with Prince Harry was much briefer than I had hoped.

As we shook hands, my vision blurred, and I could not say a word. Fortunately, Wayne stepped in and, giving me an arm to hang onto, said, "I think what you are doing for Britain's injured servicemen and women is fantastic, and it's a great honour to meet you, particularly in such a remarkable place." I managed to support my wobbly legs long enough for a photo before the Prince boarded the plane with the rest of his team. He wished me good luck and told me his grandmother, the

Queen, had said he must be home for Christmas!

It was a real privilege to meet a member of the royal family for the first time at the South Pole, despite my making a real hash of it. I didn't intend to impress, but I would have been more communicative had I not tried to show off the Polar Cycle in such a hurry.

Spotting Emil in his truck a few metres away, I trudged toward him, climbed weakly into the passenger seat, and collapsed. "You don't look too good, Maria," said Emil. I could not open my eyes, and Emil realised immediately that I was suffering from altitude sickness. I had assumed wrongly that as I was physically and mentally fit, I would have no altitude issues at all. How wrong I was. My system just couldn't cope. I'd read about the effects which could lead to cerebral oedema, a swelling of the brain caused by an increase in blood flow due to lack of oxygen—a severe condition that can kill in a matter of hours.

Concerned about my condition, Emil asked one of the doctors from the Walking with the Wounded team to check me over. "The only chance for her to get better is to drive to sea level as fast as possible," he urged. Wayne nodded in support and hurriedly helped Emil load the Polar Cycle onto the back of the truck.

The two vehicles moved in close convoy for 19 hours, traversing the crevasse-filled terrain to descend to sea level and my starting location at the continent's edge. Throughout most of that trip, I was plagued by severe symptoms of altitude sickness.

The Arctic trucks have been adapted in every way to cope with the environment and even allow for re-fuelling on the move, simply with the flick of a switch. They were incredible vehicles.

I stared out the window into the endless whiteness that seemed to compound my throbbing headache. I tried to rest my head, but it made the throbbing worse. I lay back on the truck seat, falling asleep intermittently and occasionally gazing at Emil. I hadn't even managed to meet Torfi, the second vehicle's driver.

I wondered what Emil would think of me. Would I be fit enough to start my expedition? We didn't really know each other, and I felt I needed to explain my commitment to this expedition, but all I could do was withdraw from the overwhelming feelings of sickness. I had planned to rest and refuel during this nineteen-hour journey but hadn't accounted for the possibility of this altitude sickness, and I was far from ready to begin the most incredible adventure of my life.

The truck bumped on, its engine noise compounding my headache. A large sastrugi field slowed our journey, and the truck was thrown viciously from side to side as it ploughed through the jagged ice. I couldn't believe what I was seeing. This was it. This was what I had been waiting to see for four years. Despite being in no condition to start, I was filled with an overpowering urge to get going.

After 12 hours of driving, Emil pointed out the outline of the Transantarctic Mountain Range in the distance. Wearily opening my eyes, I gazed through the windscreen at the mountain tops protruding from the ice and snow ahead. They spanned as far as my sore, tired eyes could see in both directions. Initially, I thought, 'Gosh, they are low.' However, as we drove quickly across the Polar Plateau, it became clear that I was only seeing the peaks of the mountains. In reality, the entire 3,000-metre mountain range lay beneath us.

As we drew closer, Emil double-checked his GPS to ensure we were approaching the mountains from the top of the Leverett Glacier. I sat bolt upright, transfixed by this enormous span of mountains, crevasses, and glaciers. My head was spinning, and I didn't know what to think. I asked Emil to stop at the first steep incline so I could step outside and check out the surface.

The snow was very deep, and my heart sank as I knew I would never get the traction I needed in such conditions. I was unwell, exhausted from lack of sleep and feeling very negative. I told myself I had not made it this far to be negative, and I was angry with myself for having the fleeting thought of giving up. Emil did his best to turn my doubts into hopes. Wayne was concerned about my condition but could only bite his lip. It was not a time for discussion.

I was relieved that Wayne was travelling in the other truck because I feared my condition could have sparked one of our heated debates. He would have tried very hard to make me feel positive, but I would have taken this as him patronising me. I would have kicked out, and the expedition would have started on a sour note.

Thankfully, I felt much better as we neared sea level on the Ross Ice Shelf. It was a great relief to see that with the prompt descent from altitude, my body reverted to the normal production of red blood cells, which helped me feel well again. Despite being tired and rather hungry, as I had not eaten for almost 24 hours, I felt remarkably okay. The adrenalin had kicked in, and now there was no stopping me.

I tried not to think about the thick layer of soft snow on the glacier, and I prayed that the likelihood of strong winds over the next few days would be enough to funnel the snow down off the glacier, exposing the ice that I needed for traction. The thought of this deep snow scared me because I'd have to put all my trust in the ice studs spread across my three wheels to hold me onto the glacier and prevent me from skidding backwards. A backwards journey at an uncontrollable speed down a 3,000-metre glacier would be the horrific but inevitable result.

Emil and I kept a close eye on the GPS in the truck, reading our coordinates out to each other as if for reassurance. As we got closer and closer to the marker at the continent's edge, my excitement bubbled, rapidly followed by a cold surge of dread deep in the pit of my stomach. "Are you sure this GPS is accurate?" I questioned, pointing to the device on the dashboard. I scrambled for my handheld GPS for a second opinion, but it had fallen into a crack between the door and the seat. I wanted to double-check everything. "We're almost there, Maria," Emil reassured me.

"It feels like we've travelled way beyond the glacier and are out on the ice shelf," I continued.

Emil lifted his hand to his GPS and tilted it a little more towards him. He passed no further comment. "I hope he knows what he's talking about," I thought. Emil had not been to this side of Antarctica before, so it was also a new experience for him. Luckily, our GPS positions correlated, so I trusted that technology was telling the truth.

During the last hours, I had visualised my journey back to the Pole, not in the truck, but alone on the Polar Cycle. I realised I'd need two days to cross the Ross Ice Shelf, provided the weather was kind. This would allow me time to get into my cycling routine and focus on the job in hand before facing the nightmare glacier.

At the forefront of my mind was the fact that the other cyclists, now just the American and Spaniard, had taken the traditional, safer, longer route and were now three weeks into their journey. I took this competition very seriously as we were all fighting for a world first. Even though they had chosen the longer route, I couldn't take anything for granted. At this point, none of us could predict what would happen. Variables like the weather and the conditions en route were unknown. Deep, soft snow was a killer for any wheeled vehicle; even the Arctic trucks had their limits. Our individual abilities would weigh heavily on the balance of the competition, and the only hints I had about the fitness of these two competitors were from internet blogs.

As I had kept my expedition secret, I probably knew more about them than they knew about me. I wondered about their physical and mental strengths. Who would put in the longest days cycling, who would sit out a moderate snowstorm and who would attempt to battle through it? Cycling on opposite sides of Antarctica meant we would experience different weather, and luck would play a big part. We shared a long list of potential practical problems, including bursting tyre tubes, chains that could snap, frames that could become brittle in the extreme cold, and lubrication that could freeze.

During my bicycle journey on Lake Baikal, I carried a printed photo of the lake's northern region, marking the endpoint of the race. This image served as my objective, and daily, I would take it out of my pocket to remind myself of the goal and justify the pain and hardship I was enduring. Having the visual representation to look at proved to be a significant motivator. I also carried a picture of my sister's children, Luca and Anya. These images all helped to motivate me and finish the job I had to do. I now tightly grasped an image of the South Pole Station to reinforce my focus and determination.

I couldn't believe that after four years of meticulous planning and preparation, I was on the brink of beginning my journey at a particularly unique starting point—the juncture where Antarctica's icy landscape merges with the frozen ocean. This point is delineated by a wooden stake driven into the ice, a marker set each year by American scientists from McMurdo Station.

We decided to camp 200 metres north of the post because I wanted to be 100% sure that I was on the coastline and that there was free-flowing water beneath me. I didn't talk to anyone and focused on getting myself expedition-ready. I didn't want any comments, advice or conversation anymore, as it was too late to make changes, and I had to remain focused. I had to face the challenge independently and have the courage of my conviction. Everything I'd spent months and years thinking so deeply through was now coming together. What I was sure of was that I'd put my all into making it a success.

We set up camp, and Emil and Torfi disappeared inside their tent to catch up on sleep after the mammoth drive. I could not relax with the thoughts of the other competitors in my head, and I only slept for a short while.

As I stepped outside, a biting wind cut into my cheeks. I gazed across the vast white expanse toward the sea but saw no water, only 600 kilometres of pure ice and snow. I couldn't believe I was standing on the Ross Ice Shelf—remote, wild and genuinely wonderful. I wanted to capture the moment in my mind and remember it for the rest of my life.

Wayne had risen at the same time to support me at the start, and he could see in my eyes that it was business now. Our relationship was subconsciously and temporarily put on hold, and he knew he must deal with me very carefully. We lifted the Polar Cycle from the truck and began attaching all six panniers. Wayne knew the drill as well as I did, as he'd watched me go through the same routine many times. He understood that now it was my time, and he was gentle and supportive as he taped all my fuel bottles onto the frame of the Polar Cycle using bright yellow gaffer tape. I was buzzing around impatiently as all I wanted to do was set off.

There was no sign of Emil or Torfi, so I asked Wayne to thank them for their speedy driving down to the coast. There was little time to chat. I gave Wayne an icy kiss goodbye, climbed onboard the Polar Cycle and headed towards the post in the ice. I didn't want to consider the 'what ifs' and 'buts.' I didn't want to question my ability. I could not control the weather; from now on, my only focus was cycling to the South Pole. I suspended all my fears so they didn't interfere with this important moment.

I stopped briefly at the wooden stake which marked my start position. "You can do this," Wayne said, "but before you start we need to make it official."

He pulled out a marker pen and wrote White Ice Cycle December 17, 2013, along with my name on the post. It was a significant moment, and I felt a mixture of excitement and cold reality. I had a race to win and a mission to stay alive. The goal was straightforward, but everything leading up to it was unpredictable.

I'd instructed Wayne and Emil to stay behind and out of sight for the duration of the expedition. We had previously discussed being supported, but I was determined to attempt this alone. From now on, their only role would be to take the occasional photograph and observe from afar.

The Ross Ice Shelf is the largest ice cap in Antarctica, covering 487,000 square kilometres and 800 kilometres across—about the size of Spain. It was discovered on January 28, 1841, by British explorer Sir James Clark Ross, who led an expedition to Antarctica. He named it the "Great Ice Barrier," as it prevented his ships, HMS Erebus and HMS Terror, from going further south.

As I gazed out over the ice at the panorama around me, all I could see were mounds of undulating snow drifts stretching away into nothingness. The horizon around me melted into the sky above. The temperature at sea level was a mild minus 15 degrees Celsius but the wind was on the stronger side of comfortable. It created a wave effect as the snow particles blew consistently in fluffy ripples over the surface of the ice.

I squinted in the direction of the distant McMurdo Station, hoping to catch a glimpse of a smoke plume from Mount Erebus, the southernmost active volcano on Earth. Although it was out of sight, a sense of warmth swelled inside me, knowing it was first ascended in 1908 by Professor Sir T.W. Edgeworth David, a Welshman from St. Fagans near Cardiff—just a few miles from where I live.

Over fifty metres beneath the ice on which I stood was the Ross Sea, bordered by the Southern Ocean, the world's most treacherous stretch of water. A low-lying, thick layer of cloud hovered above the ice, giving the endless, barren panorama an eerie feel. From here, I was to embark on my mission to prove that it was possible to cycle the whole way to the South Pole from the edge of the Antarctic continent. If successful, I would be the only woman to hold a significant polar world first. Unlike most start lines I had stood on, this one had no other competitors; I was well and truly on my own.

I set off into the blinding whiteness with determination, and after thirty minutes of cycling, I had the urge to gaze back at the distant trucks and our camp. At the last minute, I stopped myself. I needed to have my complete focus ahead, due south all the time. Each pedal rotation took me further away from safety but closer to the Pole. My journey had well and truly begun.

I settled into the moment and concentrated on maximising every revolution of the cycle wheels. My legs were strong and fresh, and I worked them hard. After training for hundreds of hours on the Polar Cycle in preparation for this expedition, I was well used to the position and sat comfortably. I was not a trike cyclist, but I had grown to enjoy the position, and the back support was a great lever for my thighs—the strongest part of my anatomy.

My panniers on either side of the Polar Cycle were securely fastened, travelled well, did not get in the way of my cycling and easily supported my 55 kilograms of kit. My feet sat snuggly in my polar boots, supported firmly on the large pedals with a heel rest and toe strap to hold them in place. My hands were kept warm with wool base layer gloves topped up by the soft, fluffy interior of the pogies, which were oversized mitts attached permanently to the handlebars of my Polar Cycle. I could steer and operate the brakes comfortably.

As a bonus to the repetitive cycling, I had placed some snacks inside the pogies so I could pull out a treat to boost my reserves. I soon realised, though, that the fur inside the pogies was beginning to stick to my sweet collection, so from day one, I had to accustom myself to Antarctica-tailored snacks!

I kept myself busy absorbing my surroundings when I wasn't snacking on sweets. Ice hundreds of metres thick lay in all directions around me. It covered the land to the south, including the Transantarctic Mountains, and to the north, it spanned over the ocean. Occasionally, to my right, I could see the far-off Transantarctic Mountains peeking through and gentle rises in the snow that transformed into small, wind-sculpted mountains as I cycled nearer. These formations were randomly yet exquisitely shaped by the wind accompanying the massive glaciers that flowed from the mountains toward the sea. I was travelling on an uphill gradient of between one to six per cent, and I knew it would only get more challenging.

My speed averaged five kilometres per hour, but I regularly faced deep snow mounds, causing my front wheels to sink and my back wheel to spin. I used my hands on the wheels to free myself and was soon on my way again. I regularly glanced at my GPS bearing and noted my uphill journey was well underway. I had imagined this first section of the expedition to be the easiest. It would be the warmest part of my journey, the least steep and given it was an ice cap, it would have far less snow and more exposed ice.

My pattern for the day became my mantra. I pedalled hard for an hour without allowing myself to sweat, then rested for a strictly time-controlled three-minute break. My break involved stepping off the Polar Cycle to give my body a change of position and to promote the all-important blood circulation. I knelt downwind so the Polar Cycle would act as a windbreak while I took a brief rest. I fumbled with my gloves to find my thermos flask and, at the same time, took a handful of energy snacks from my bumbag on my front and threw them in the direction of my mouth. I soon learnt that I had to consume my liquid lunch within the first three hours of making it because, after that, it would be frozen solid. Life in Antarctica was going to be very tough, and taking for granted homely comforts such as warmth, food, and water and going to the toilet would be a constant challenge.

I had to accept that I would wear the same clothes for an undefined amount of time—two, three or even four weeks. I knew from experience that the discomfort of wearing the same clothes comes around day three, and then it seems to get better, or rather less important. I tried to envisage my body would clean itself, though I knew it was only an illusion and I would have to accept the inevitable stench and uncomfortable stickiness that comes with poor hygiene. The only consolation was that nobody else was around to suffer it.

I consoled myself with the decision that the first few days needed to be more about getting into a good routine and adapting to life in Antarctica instead of clocking up the miles. It was too early to make mistakes that could threaten the rest of the expedition. My competitive streak softened slightly as I focused purely on my well-being. I needed to be totally at ease with my performance before I could think about other people.

Nevertheless, I realised early on that I had made two huge errors, which, in retrospect, were blatantly ridiculous. I had chosen to wear a cycle helmet to hold my full-face visor in place, not for head protection but as an efficient wind barrier that removed the need for goggles that would steam up.

Mistakenly, thinking of the possibility of a whiteout, I had chosen a transparent visor instead of a tinted one, and therefore, I needed to wear sunglasses underneath it to prevent snow blindness. The neck scarf that kept my neck and chin warm caused the sunglasses to steam up constantly. I giggled at how strange I must look cycling across Antarctica in a standard cycle helmet with huge wing nuts at each temple to hold the useless visor in place! I even went to a motorbike specialist to source the visor, and they gave it to me for free.

My second mistake caused me bitter disappointment because initially, I thought I had been inventive. Before leaving for Antarctica, I was given a roll of Thinsulate material that I used to make jackets for all my electrical items, such as my satellite phone, mobile phone and GPS, to keep them warm and prolong battery life. I had overlooked that because these items were switched off, they did not produce heat, and the jacket kept them cold. I had confused creativity with practicality, so I resorted to my usual method for prolonging battery life in extreme cold conditions by shoving anything electrical in my socks, pants, and bra. My body proved to be an excellent radiator.

I set off in cloudy conditions, but the sun's warmth soon penetrated the grey sky just behind my left shoulder, then rose high in front of me like an expanding ball of fire. Later, with the sun glaring straight into my visor, the cloud broke to create curling, smoky whispers.

I was only one day into the expedition, but I already felt comfortable about the performance of my Polar Cycle. So far, it rode well and proved to be the right cycle for the job. I revelled in my solitude, indulging in the breathtaking panoramas of vast nothingness surrounding me from every angle.

I could not believe that I was really in Antarctica. While I tried to concentrate on the present, my mind rolled back to when I started my adventurous life in the Sahara Desert, competing in the Marathon des Sables. As I recalled the intense heat of the Sahara, it helped me cope with the intense cold in a comforting way. I had no clue then about how I would cope with the heat and whether my body would be up to the challenge, and now I was feeling the same in opposite conditions. I was comforted by the fact that I knew I thrived better in the cold.

In the Sahara, my contrasting concerns were whether I would suffer sunstroke and dehydration or even break a leg as I pounded through the deep, soft sand. As my wheels sank into the deep snow here in Antarctica, it felt like I was sinking into the desert sand. My careful routine of ensuring every grain of sand was removed from my shoes and socks as I passed through checkpoints was the lifeline to my success in the Sahara. It cost me an extra 60 seconds at each checkpoint, but as a result, I finished the race with not a single blister and in a peak physical state compared to many others around me, who were hobbling and stumbling over the finish line.

Now, here in the snow, my feet were again a top priority. Sitting in a recumbent position was not conducive to delivering blood to my feet, so I had to take regular breaks to jump up and down and ensure that frostbite did not set in.

I have always suffered from cold hands and feet, and after a handshake, people often commented about my cold hands. To me, it felt normal as I always felt warm inside. My feet had taken a hammering in the Last Wild Race in Patagonia, where I'd experienced the early onset of frostbite, and I'd already lost a toenail on the big toe of my right foot. I was also suffering from a long-standing fungal infection, which I'd not taken time to treat. Fortunately, the cold conditions gave some light relief from the aggravating itching.

I recalled my concern about route finding in the Sahara and remembered the odd explanation on the start line by the organiser, who had a strong French accent. "You think you lost, then follow person in front," she shouted. I had no such luxury now.

I did know that looking after myself was the most critical part of this expedition, and I was reminded of an OTC officer's words: "Always look after number one." Initially, I considered this selfish, but now it made sense. Antarctica is an unforgiving place; any mistake would cost me the expedition and possibly my life. If I had any sign of hypothermia, I would have to stop, put up my tent quickly and get my stove running. If I ran out of water or was injured or ill, I'd have to do the same thing in record time. Heat was fundamental to this expedition, and I needed to keep my body temperature at 37 degrees Celsius. The only two ways of achieving this were through physical exhaustion or powering up my stove.

The pressure of competition meant I had to be clear about how far to push and when it was essential to stop, bearing in mind it would take a further hour to set up my tent and heat up my stove. I concluded that the fewer the tent stops, the more time I'd spend cycling, and the race would be mine.

# 13. Life Inside My Little Red Tent

"Precision is vital when you have very little"

The Antarctic wilderness is tantalisingly beautiful yet worryingly vicious. I basked in its vastness and glowed with pride at having the opportunity to be there. Seconds later, the sensation of glory shrunk, and I felt myself evaporate into a solitary speck on the Antarctic ice.

My solitary status felt unreal but somehow comforting. I wanted it no other way. This was my mission, and from now on, success was my responsibility. The team had done everything possible to help me prepare, and I now had to follow through. Everything depended on the strength of my mind and my legs. I repeated to myself numerous times. 'I'm the first person to cycle to the South Pole.' 'I'm the first person to cycle to the South Pole.' I was desperate to turn this hope into reality. The sun was still high in the sky behind my right shoulder, and the temperature dropped dramatically. The wind was picking up, and it was time to think about setting up camp for my first night alone in Antarctica.

I had covered just over 40 kilometres and was delighted with my progress, but 12 hours of cycling had made me weary. 'That's normal,' I told myself, still turning the pedals to find the perfect spot. Every spot looked similar, differentiated only by the way the snow lay. There were deeper mounds in some places and firmer snow in others. I scanned the ground continuously to find a suitable position for my tent. The wind was building, so it would be a testing time to pitch my tent and prevent it from blowing away. I knew the drill well but ran the whole procedure through my mind again before dismounting the Polar Cycle.

My bright red tent protected me from the harsh elements. It measured two metres by one metre and was simple and uncomplicated; inside, everything had its place. I had chosen my Hilleberg tent out of many tent brands and settled only for the best. It had already proved perfect for the job in my previous cold weather expeditions. It was light, easy to assemble and dismantle, and my best friend. Fortunately, I was experienced in setting up camp in extreme conditions and a bizarre sense of homeliness set in as I climbed into it night after night.

My tent routine started when I stopped cycling and stopped when I slept. On average, it took three hours, and it was essential that I had energy left at the end of my hard day of cycling to grapple with the necessity of eating and staying fit and alive to tackle the extremes of the following day.

I finally succumbed to any old spot to pitch my tent since all spots were blankets of whiteness, and I wasn't sure what I was looking for in the first place. The moment I stopped pedalling, I put on an extra layer of clothing to keep warm. The temperature was minus 18 degrees Celsius with a strong wind. I didn't feel particularly cold, but I had only a few seconds to ensure I maintained the heat my working body had generated as I prepared for the evening ritual. I realised that time was limited and urgency was paramount as I pulled on my thick over jacket, which enveloped my tired, aching body in comforting layers of down and a second pair gloves to preserve the protection I had had from the pogies. Keeping my hands warm was a top priority as they were vital for tent building.

Snug and warm in my gloves and jacket, I moved quickly on to removing the bungee cords that held my tent onto the rear rack of my Polar Cycle. With an extra layer of gloves, this was a frustrating task. I had to constantly take the second pair of gloves on and off to make progress and ensure I did not freeze in the process. I knew the procedure would be even more frustrating on the Polar Plateau, with extra mittens to ward off the cold.

I had erected my tent many times at home and even completed it blindfolded. As I stood there in the white wilderness, it was a very different story. With the tent bag squashed firmly between my feet, I tugged on the pull cord to release the tent, stuffing the bag down the front of my jacket so it didn't blow away. The wind was beating into my back, and I tried to stop the tent from flickering wildly like an escaped kite, but it was hard to control the flapping. In that wild moment of frenzy, there was so much to coordinate. I spun around hurriedly to check that nothing had blown away and stood for a moment, lost in time as the noise of the flapping tent whistled even louder, almost drowning the now ferocious wind that had picked up since I had stopped cycling. I had to learn to balance my cold weather panic with patience. I clipped the carabiner from the tent cord to a loop on the side of my polar boots to ensure I had a secure hold. Without my tent, I was doomed.

I scraped away the soft snow until I found a firm base below. I fumbled frantically, trying to insert the tent poles into the reinforced plastic sleeves as the dome-shaped tent started to take shape. I piled the snow up on the valances with my spade to stop the draft and wind blowing snow under the tent while sleeping. The deep, soft snow was light and fluffy with little moisture and provided poor resistance to the elements, so there was a risk that the tent pegs would pull out and the snow on the valances would blow off.

My tiny tent was a welcome respite from the day's struggle. Diving inside brought an instant smile to my face, though I had to be careful not to catch the studs in my boots on the thin, base fabric of the tent. I pulled out my GPS and studied my course. I carried graphs that displayed the elevation profile of my climb. The steepest slope I had ascended today was at a 6% gradient. Tomorrow, this gradient was expected to increase to 8%, and over the following two or three days, it would further steepen to 25%. I had already struggled cycling through areas with deep snow on inclines with a 6% gradient. I tried to imagine a 25% gradient and realised I would only stand a chance if the glacier surface was clean ice. Then float would not be a problem, and the ice studs in my tyres should provide enough grip to get me up.

I had very low gearing that would allow me to churn away on the pedals, and even though I'd only make minuscule progress, at least it would be some progress. I prayed that the wind would channel strongly down the glacier for the next few days to blow away the top layer of softer snow. Positive thinking made me feel good, even if the likelihood of this perfect scenario was slim.

The tent was just large enough for me, plus two of my pannier bags, making for a very homely environment. At five foot ten inches tall, my head and feet almost touched each end, and with the pannier bags on one side, there was little remaining room to manoeuvre, let alone be comfortable. I couldn't sit up straight, so all my tasks were undertaken in a half-lying down position. This was uncomfortable, and my back soon began to ache. At this point, I was reminded of one small annoyance I should have sorted out following my expedition in Siberia. The only position in the tent where I could sit almost upright was directly underneath the door zip of the tent, but every time I moved my head, I would brush up against it, and it would become tangled in my hair. Despite having tied my hair back, every time I moved, I had to spend a further few minutes yanking a clump of hair out of the zip to free myself. I resorted to wearing my headscarf to relieve the problem.

With my Thermorest fully inflated and the warmth of my big down sleeping bag underneath me, I set out to establish the most effective water-making process possible. During the Lake Baikal race, I learnt to time and measure every stage of water making with perfect precision. It was essential to have a small amount of water left over in my flask after each day when I stopped to set up camp. I unzipped my pannier bag and pulled out my cooking equipment and food. It was time for my cooking ritual to begin.

I poured approximately half an inch of my leftover water from the day into my pan, bringing it almost to a boil. I crumbled gently into the pan a combination of powdered snow and tiny pieces of ice that I had excavated from the entrance of my tent. It was vitally important to gauge the temperature of the water as the aim was to keep it just below boiling point. Too much snow and ice reduced the water temperature and took much longer to boil. Too little meant I was wasting water through steam. Both scenarios required more precious fuel to make the same amount of water. It was a fine art, and I was passionate about getting it right.

I reflected on how one of the early Norwegian explorers, Fridtjof Nansen, had developed his perfect formula epitomised in the cooker that took his name. His stove allowed explorers to heat their food at the same time as melting snow for water. An enclosed burner with a cylindrical aluminium vessel that held two cooking pots, one within another, allowed the heat to pass around both. I didn't have his equipment, but I prided myself on being as methodical as Nansen would have been. I predicted I'd use one-quarter of a bottle of fuel each day, so I had five bottles strapped to the Polar Cycle, enough to last twenty days.

I recalled my experience back home when I failed at my first attempt at lighting my stove. Knowing that lighters don't tend to work well at altitude, I brought a collection of fire-igniting options, including lighters, normal matches, waterproof matches, and a fire striker. As I struck a match against the box, it lit up immediately. This was beginner's luck I thought, as I stowed away my other fire-lighting options.

The challenge of water making took up most of my tent time, and to use only a quarter of a litre of fuel, my stove had to be at maximum productivity all the time. After the first pan reached boiling point, I added 300 millilitres of my 500 millilitres of boiled water to my mushroom soup and then promptly zipped up the packet to keep the heat in whilst the soup started to rehydrate. I now had a choice with the remaining 200 millilitres of boiling water. I needed 300 millilitres for my main meal, but I also wanted to make a cup of hot chocolate. I needed 300 millilitres for my pudding, plus 500 millilitres for the thermos flask I used for my morning porridge, ensuring it was pre-melted, saving me time in the morning, and 300 millilitres for my hydration system to drink at night. It was a mathematical nightmare!

I spooned the piping hot mushroom soup into my mouth and made the most of its warmth trickling down my throat. At the same time, in my other hand, I had a shovel to break up the ice that lay in my tent porch to ensure I always had fresh snow and ice to add to my simmering pan of perfection. My half-lying down posture added to the awkwardness of the situation. Swilling down mushroom soup and hot chocolate without spilling it everywhere became a newly acquired skill. Nevertheless, there was something about this routine that gave me great satisfaction.

I lay down briefly to relieve the pain in my back, which had started from sitting bent over my stove, and I felt pleased with myself for surviving the start of yet another mammoth task. I felt my cooking routine could be improved if I had more space, but I didn't have the option of giving up my beloved tent for a larger model just yet.

By the time I was halfway through my mushroom soup, my next pan was nearly boiling. It was decision time again. My main meal—a choice between chicken curry, spaghetti Bolognese, beef and vegetables, salmon and potato or my favourite, beef stroganoff—was simplified by the fact that I had pre-packed twenty-four-hour ration bags.

Before pulling the pack out of the pannier, I tried to guess what was for dinner, knowing I would be disappointed if it was the same as last night. We enjoyed a spaghetti Bolognese as our last meal together. Luckily, this evening, it was chicken curry. With a varying degree of enthusiasm, I added the 300 millilitres of water to the food, zipped up the pouch, and allowed it to stand in my sleeping bag for the required ten minutes.

After my main course, I took a break from the culinary ritual to focus on my electrical department, which lay in its place to the right of my feet. This was the first time that I had experienced 24-hour daylight. The brightness inside my tent powered a solar panel, which topped up my tracking device. This was my lifeline with its emergency call function. It showed only 21% battery life, but it excited me to watch the sun work its magic and charge it up free of charge. I still had to carry batteries to power my GPS, radio and iPhone.

The sound of simmering water brought me back to the task at hand. I plugged my tracking device back into the power source, carefully poured the water into my thermos flask, and set my pan to heat for the fourth time. With the water production still in full flow, it was now time for dessert. The choice was either chocolate chip pudding or apple and custard.

During past expeditions, I learnt that if I didn't rehydrate the apple and custard sufficiently, it made for an unpleasant powdery custard that spent all night stuck in the back of my throat. The chocolate chip pudding, however, was delightful, and although I had spent the day indulging in various chocolates, I relished this dessert. Tonight, however, I had to settle for the culinary challenge of apple and custard.

Topping up the disappointment of my dessert choice was the fact that my spork now carried the remnants of mushroom soup and chicken curry. An acrid aftertaste of my earlier meals framed the sweet, bitter taste of powdered apples and custard. "Ughh! Oh, for a tasty meal back home," I said. I couldn't believe that I was pining after normal food on the first night of my expedition, although I had been on expedition rations since leaving the relative comfort of Novolazarevskaya Station four days earlier.

Finally, I was on the last leg of water-making, and this pan didn't even need to boil, as it was drinking water for my hydration system for the night. I lay back in my sleeping bag, relieved.

My next job was teeth cleaning. I reached for my toothbrush, which promptly fell out of my mouth, as I scrambled dreamily back into a seated position to reach my toothpaste from the first aid bag. The feeling of minty breath was heavenly, eliminating that stifling, furry feeling inside my mouth that had come from constantly picking on snacks throughout the day.

It was almost time to sleep, but one of my last jobs had to be performed with great care. I needed to relieve my full bladder, so I prepared myself for some precision peeing, as there was no way I was now going to put all my clothes back on and go outside. Besides, if I opened the tent door, the precious heat I had created from my kitchen would escape and be lost to the icy world.

I reached for my clearly marked 'wee' bottle. There was no room for error here because any mistake would turn my home into a hovel, and I had no plans for dealing with wee in my sleeping bag. Luckily, I had plenty of practice with the technique during my Siberian expedition. I knelt up on my knees, bent double due to the severe lack of headroom and then forced the bottle in between my legs, ensuring it was nestling securely in place, before waiting for an extended amount of time for my brain to allow my body to let go sufficiently to permit me to pass water neatly, straight into the bottle. Seeing my sleeping bag lying just below me was unnatural, so I momentarily shut my eyes and pictured a toilet. Success! With the lid screwed on firmly, I pushed the bottle to the bottom of my sleeping bag to keep it warm so that I could dispose of it correctly the following morning in a dug-out hole.

Within a radius of 100 kilometres of the South Pole, you must carry all excrement with you, but as I was outside that limit, I could dispense with it myself.

The final pre-requisite before sleep was a quick clean. With limited wet wipes, only four per day to be precise, this task could only be carried out one way – from top to bottom!

"Oh shit!" I screamed. During my self-cleaning ritual, I'd managed to kneel on my Spork, an all-in-one plastic spoon, knife and fork which I had left lying on the top of my sleeping bag. It was my only tool for scraping food out of my food pouch, and I'd snapped it right at the base of the handle.

24 hours of daylight dramatically affected the temperature inside my tent. The red canvas absorbed the sun's rays, and my body heat and the heat left over from cooking enhanced the temperature inside my tent to a comfortable 10 degrees Celsius. My minus-fifty-degree-rated sleeping bag was far too warm, and I decided to sleep on top of it this evening. I stripped down to my bra and knickers and found it hard to believe I was in Antarctica, lying on ice millions of years old and fathoms deep, in just my underwear!

At rest at last, I considered how little I missed the ring of my 'phone, the glare of my laptop or the constant pressure to be something or somewhere. I was simply me, totally alone. It made me think long and hard about how material excesses overshadowed my life and often created unnecessary pressures. I had had enough pressure over the last three hours simply trying to stay alive! I glanced at my watch; it was 03.12 GMT. Time seemed almost irrelevant as I managed my day by the sun's position. It was a wonderful feeling.

I woke in fits and starts throughout the night, sometimes to turn over and other times gasping for water. I had woken three times already from thirst – it must have been because of that sticky apple and custard. I drank all the contents of my hydration system during the night.

Thankfully, my recurring nightmares for the last six months about climbing the Leverett Glacier did not surface that night. Soon, it would be a reality. As I opened my eyes, I knew that if I made good headway on the second day, I'd make it to the base of the glacier. It was time to begin my morning routine, and I focused on the tasks ahead. I set myself a one-hour time limit until departure, unable to tell if I was rested or delusional.

Within minutes of waking, I put my stove on to rehydrate my porridge. Even though I had consumed over 3,000 calories the night before and had only a few hours of rest, my body was ready to take on more. Breakfast has always been my favourite meal of the day, and today was no exception. The porridge also had some raisins in it, and the stodgy texture, for some reason, brought a smile to my face. Maybe I'd had a good night's sleep after all.

I began to pack away my electrical department while searching for my toothbrush, ready to brush my teeth after breakfast. I needed a little more water to top up my thermos flask before turning off the stove. I added a liquid lunch meal to my thermos, which was vanilla-flavoured today. It was a great product because one litre instantly gave me 800 calories of energy, even though I had to consume it all within the first few hours to prevent it from freezing solid. I had to adapt my appetite to the weather conditions.

After a quick brush of my teeth, it was time to layer on my clothing and abandon the warmth of my sleeping bag. I'd crawled back into it during the night as the temperature had dipped and the warmth created by my stove had dispersed.

I packed my sleeping bag away into its compression sack without allowing myself to think of what the day ahead might bring. I used my body weight to extract the air from my sleeping mat and checked everything was packed in the correct pockets of my pannier bag so that, in an instant, I would know where everything was. Fortunately, in Cape Town, I'd labelled each pocket on my pannier bags, which proved an invaluable aid to progress in the sleep-deprived state I was now living in. My headscarf had fallen off during the night, so once again, I snagged my hair in the tent zip.

The time had come to face the white world outside. With socks and boots now on, I sat with my feet in the porch of my tent, dropping into the small pit from my snow and ice excavations the previous night. I kept telling myself that the sooner I got on with it, the sooner I would reach the South Pole. With one final deep breath, I unzipped the outer door of my tent, and the freezing Antarctic air rushed in, colliding against the warmth of my body.

# 14. The Dreaded Leverett Glacier

*"The nightmare that once was, becomes reality"*

I packed away my kit and collapsed my tent, grabbing the flapping canvas as I stuffed it into the tent bag. I knew the glacier ahead of me was steep, and the climb would tax every inch of my body, but I told myself it was necessary pain that I had to endure on my journey through the Transantarctic Mountain Range from the coast of Antarctica to the South Pole.

The Transantarctic Mountain Range extends across the continent from Cape Adare in northern Victoria Land to Coats Land, dividing east and west Antarctica. Many glaciers poured out of the mountain range, and I had chosen the Leverett Glacier as my gateway to the South Pole. It helped to know that this glacier's incline was less than some of the others that flowed off the Polar Plateau.

The snow on the mountains, glistening in the sun, was occasionally punctuated by exposed dark peaks where the snow had fallen or blown away. All at once, my thoughts of gradients and beautiful views were interrupted when I heard a distant thud that echoed towards me, followed by an increasingly loud roar. My blood did whatever blood does when it makes your spine tingle as, looking to my right, I witnessed a huge wall of snow sheer away from the side of the mountain and cascade down the slopes, producing a massive white plume. Avalanches can be unpredictable and deadly, and to see them speeding down the mountainside before my eyes was deeply unsettling.

I dwelled briefly on the frightening knowledge that the human body is three times denser than avalanche debris and will sink quickly. Once buried, bodily movement is nearly impossible, and you die quickly of suffocation as the snow hardens.

Avalanche after avalanche powering down the mountains throughout the day gnawed into my fears about my safety and the glacier climb ahead. I was determined to reach the base of the glacier before pitching my tent for a second night. Although tired, I had already cycled thirty-one kilometres and was determined to continue and at least tackle the lower section of the climb.

I was travelling in a wonderland. It was overwhelming and surreal, and I could hardly comprehend where I was. My perception of distance was confused. The scale, magnificence and emptiness of the mountain range to my right grew closer as I pedalled. I thought about how Scott and Amundsen would have felt over a hundred years ago and how they would have tackled the unknown. The Beardmore glacier that Captain Scott had chosen and the Axel Heiberg glacier that Roald Amundsen had tackled were steeper but shorter in distance than the Leverett Glacier. They would have arrived at the mountain base with dogs and ponies. I was about to arrive alone, with my unusual-looking, untested Polar Cycle.

I had chosen a route that modern expeditioners had barely touched, but at least I'd had the benefit of researching maps and photographs of the area, neither of which Scott nor Amundsen would have had access to. Nevertheless, I was petrified.

For the first time on my journey, I began to doubt the strength in my thighs, which I had worked so hard to build up over the last year. I took some comfort in the fact that my 985 watts of maximum power, which I had produced in my fitness testing, would help me. However, testing my legs in a controlled environment was no comparison to testing them on a glacier in Antarctica at minus 40 degrees Celsius.

The sameness of each headland confused my actual position, and I kept miscalculating my arrival at the base of the Leverett Glacier. I was not looking at my GPS at this stage as the overpowering view of the mountain range captivated my mind, and I was leaving it to instinct to work out my position. Tears of frustration began to stream down my cheeks. They froze instantly in contact with the icy air. I lifted my face mask to try and protect my cheeks. They felt hot from panic and exertion, then instantly cold from the bitter breeze that blew light snow across the icy plain of the Ross Ice Shelf. I must pedal on.

At last, the magnificent glacier came into view, and I knew there was no other way to turn. If I was to reach the South Pole, I had to climb it. I had studied the gradients of the glacier, metre by metre, and I knew there were five very steep sections of up to 25% gradient. As the early evening remained clear, with only a slight headwind, conditions were so good that I had to push on. If the wind picked up, it would channel down the glacier, and I could be in trouble.

My tyres were rumbling over hard-packed ice, with the occasional layer of soft snow blown from a snowdrift. The strong winds that regularly channelled down the glacier exposed the ice, making the possibility of pitching a tent more and more difficult. I feared I did not have sufficient ice screws to hold my tent on pure ice in a severe storm. The lack of snow would mean I would have to dig up huge blocks of ice to lay on the valances to keep my tent secured to the ground.

Even now, as I began to climb, I was unsure if I was really on the glacier. The surface appearance of the snow was the only clue I had to go by. The snow was lying evenly all around me, and I took this as an indication that the snow was lying on the smooth surface of the glacier. I glanced hurriedly at my GPS and noted the figure -85.72 latitude and -146.31 longitude. It confirmed I had arrived at the base of the Leverett Glacier. The vast mountains around me hugged the landscape, and I felt smaller than ever in the vast wilderness.

One moment, the glacier seemed to tower down on me as angry as it had been in my nightmares, and another moment, the ice looked smooth and the gradient shallow. I realised that my vision was deceiving me, and my ability to calculate depth was impaired. The glacier stretched 3,000 metres above sea level in an endless tail of ice that disappeared into the sky above.

I couldn't visualise the height, the incline or the top of the glacier, which I so desperately wanted to reach. I knew I had to make two ninety-degree turns to avoid a huge crevasse field halfway up the glacier. Even though we had driven down the glacier a few days earlier in the Arctic trucks, it was now all a blur. Having seen the sheer enormity of the task ahead, I had closed my eyes and laid back in the truck, thinking, I'll never be able to do this.

My thoughts started to fracture at the prospect of the climb ahead, so I forced myself to concentrate on the magnificence of my immediate surroundings. Sometimes, I had to pinch myself just in case I was dreaming. The enormity of the mountain range that surrounded me was mind-blowing and indescribable—too vast for my mind to handle. It prompted demons to pop into my mind, and I had to make a constant effort to chase them away as I pedalled on.

Out of necessity, my mind forged a survival strategy that emerged spontaneously. I visualised an invisible boundary encircling myself and the Polar Cycle in this critical, desperate moment. I call this my invisible circle, where I permit myself to focus only on things I can influence, ensuring my warmth, taking care of my body, feeding myself, and maintaining the Polar Cycle and my gear. I resolved that everything outside this circle was out of my hands and should be disregarded. I chose not to dwell on it, merely to observe it passively, seeing and hearing but not reacting. I couldn't control the avalanches, the lurking crevasses, or the fierce winds, so I refused to be consumed by 'what if' scenarios. Embracing this focused frame of mind brought me tranquillity and a comforting acceptance that, should it be my final moment, I had done all within my power until the very end.

Over the last two days, I had climbed gradients of between one and eight per cent, and I was accustomed to cycling uphill. My legs were tired but fully engaged, and I had plenty of strength left.

Until now, I had avoided using my lowest gear ring on the front wheel, as having one more ring in reserve gave me hope. The gradient was now rising to between eight and ten per cent in places. I had cycled fifty kilometres in 13 hours and twenty minutes, and my GPS revealed that I was at an altitude of 1,452 metres. That meant I had just over one thousand four hundred metres left to climb up the glacier.

Suddenly, I hit a slightly steeper section of the glacier and was forced to enter my lowest front gear ring for the first time. I dreaded this as I needed to save this gear for the most challenging inclines. I pushed on, and the pedalling became very tough indeed. As I reached 51 kilometres, I was forced to stop. I was shattered, and the thought of what lay ahead was overwhelming.

I searched for a flattish ledge in the snow and turned the Polar Cycle ninety degrees to the glacier, hauled on the parking brake and jammed the front brakes on using the straps from my pogies. I was now sitting right in the middle of the Leverett Glacier. Cold and tired, I quickly erected my tent on the ledge next to my cycle. I was pitching on ice, so I hammered my tent pegs in to provide a secure grounding. I carved out manageable blocks of Antarctic ice with my ice axe to layer on my valances for added security. It was a tough, strenuous upper-body workout that my tired body could have done without.

As I worked through my exhaustion, the routine became more comfortable. It was a calm evening, and everything seemed straightforward, which brought me a sense of relief. Life was simple on my own as I only had myself to argue with, worry about and organise.

I loved the feeling of independence. I had taken part in many adventure races throughout my life, and the most challenging aspect was dealing with the emotional highs and lows experienced by everyone in a team. I only had myself to think about and myself to blame. It was strangely uncomplicated.

That night, as every night, I rehydrated my food by melting snow over my small stove. Due to increasing altitude, I was rapidly losing my appetite, and by the time my food was ready, I didn't feel like eating. I cheered myself up using my only contact with the outside world, my satellite phone, to send a few short tweets. I wrote, "Two very tough days ahead up Leverett", "Can't believe I am camped part way up Leverett, which has been giving me nightmares", and "All I want for Christmas is to get to the top of this glacier."

I wondered how much 'farmor' my Swedish grandmother would have admired my expedition. We were very close, and when she died from Alzheimer's, I was devastated. With her very much in my heart, I decided to make the Alzheimer's Society my chosen expedition charity because it addresses the most prevalent form of dementia, which will impact one in three individuals. While I've never succeeded in raising an enormous sum of money, even a modest contribution of a few thousand pounds per expedition to this admirable organisation can make a difference. I also hoped that my tweets might encourage more donations. That night, the wind picked up suddenly and then dropped again with equal rapidity. I had been adamant in Cape Town that I needed to buy a watch so I could set an alarm to wake me up. As it turned out, I didn't use it once. I slept lightly, waking up automatically every 30 minutes to check the time and the condition of my tent. Just before pitching my tent, I'd seen some dangerous-looking crevasses about six metres from where I had been cycling. I didn't understand the behaviour of crevasses, particularly on glaciers, but I figured it would be safer to pitch above a crevasse on a glacier rather than below it. As I lay dozing, I prayed that I'd moved far enough up the glacier to be safe should the crevasse grow overnight. Unsurprisingly, my fears kept me awake for most of the night.

My night-time thirst had also returned. That evening, I hadn't taken the time to produce water for my hydration system, and I didn't want to use up my morning water in my thermos flask, so I scrambled around trying to find a small block of ice lying on the porch of my tent with my bare hands. The shock of ice on my warm fingertips was inevitable and unexpected. I found a lump of ice the size of the palm of my hand and slowly, in a sleep-deprived state, lifted it to my lips. I sucked carefully on a corner, but I was unable to extract any water from it. There was so little humidity in the air that even the ice contained little water. I sucked desperately as my lips tingled on the freezing surface. After a few minutes, I extracted a few drips to quench my thirst, allowing me to fall asleep for another temporary slumber.

With the sun now back in its morning position, it was time for me to start cycling. At the South Pole, the sun is always above the horizon in the summer and below the horizon in the winter, which means the region experiences up to 24 hours of sunlight in the summer and 24 hours of darkness in the winter.

Consequently, the sun rises and sets only twice a year—at the September and March equinox. I was still operating on UK time but cycling in the southern hemisphere's nighttime.

I gazed out from the comfort of my tent and noted that the visibility had dropped to almost nothing. Strangely, my first reaction was delight. I convinced myself that I wouldn't be able to worry if I couldn't see how steep the incline was. I packed up my panniers and tried to picture the maps and photographs I had religiously digested before the expedition. I slipped the photo of the South Pole I was carrying out of my pocket, stared at it, and kissed it. "Maria! You can do this… I'll be with you soon," I said encouragingly to myself.

It was time to traverse one of the steepest sections of the Leverett Glacier. Not only would I be cycling uphill, but I'd also be cycling at an angle as well. I had thought long and hard about this during the night and decided that if I packed more weight in the pannier on the uphill side of the slope, the possibility of the Polar Cycle tipping over might be reduced.

As I packed my tent away, I thought briefly about the other bikers attempting to claim a world first. Before I started my expedition, I had heard that they were at around 82 degrees south latitude and had travelled approximately two hundred and twenty kilometres in three weeks. They were still a long way from the Pole.

My research told me that cycling the whole way, or even most of that route, would be impossible due to the soft, deep snow. I also had to contend with soft, deep snow, but the fact that the underlying base was more compacted was a benefit.

By now, visibility had dropped to between one and two metres, so I set my GPS. I had to avoid the crevasse sections lurking in random places all over the glacier. I prayed that I could stay on track and avoid the dangers. I began pedalling in my lowest gear, which was an unnerving start to the day. It was my only option.

The alternative was to drag the Polar Cycle, which I knew was almost impossible. I had tested this option thoroughly at home, in Iceland and around the ALCI airbase. Towing the Polar Cycle, fully loaded up a steep hill was incredibly physically challenging and intensely annoying, as it didn't quite track correctly and constantly veered to the right. The spectre of this impossible task made me even more determined to cycle every inch of the way.

As I could not see the incline ahead, my only option was concentrating on one metre at a time. My speed was down to between 1 and 2.4 kilometres per hour. It would be a long, slow day of covering little distance. I started the traverse across the glacier, and the Polar Cycle, heavily loaded, began to heel over. I leant uphill with all my weight to stabilise the cycle and keep it on three wheels. Fortunately, there was only a light headwind, and traction was good, so I pushed on, repeating to myself, 'Keep the pedals turning'. There were moments when I thought the whole cycle, the panniers and my life, would tip over and be lost forever, just as in my nightmare. I told myself I must stop and put on my harness at the next opportunity.

After about forty-five minutes, I was off the traverse, and the incline became steeper. I needed to stop to attach myself physically to the Polar Cycle. I jammed on the brakes as hard as possible and climbed off, ensuring my foot landed directly behind one of the front wheels to provide further braking. I pulled out my harness from my right-hand pannier bag and fastened it around my waist before clipping it to the steering tube. This ensured it did not interfere with my pedalling. I had invested in a quick-release kayaking harness because I figured that if the Polar Cycle were to fall down a crevasse, I would need a way of releasing myself from it quickly before I fell, too.

Constant flashes of possible disasters ran through my mind, and nothing made sense. What if the Polar Cycle and all my kit were too heavy and dragged me down the crevasse before I had time to release myself? What if I didn't have time to release it? I'd then be stuck halfway up the glacier with no kit and no Polar Cycle.

The harness sat uncomfortably around my waist, so I fidgeted constantly with my clothes to accommodate its extra bulk. I had not trained at home with the harness on, and I scolded myself for overlooking the vital principle of 'always test equipment before an expedition.' As expected, I developed a sore back from the harness. As my back pushed against the seat, the quick-release toggles from the harness constantly got in the way. The batteries I had tucked into the warmth of my bra started to press into my skin uncomfortably, exacerbating the discomfort I was already feeling. I knew I couldn't remove them because the power would be lost to the cold.

The stop provided an opportunity to check my emergency kit stuffed into my jacket pockets. I'd always made a point of having my emergency communication, food and water, as well as anything that could freeze up, stowed in the relative warmth of my jacket. I had two pockets on either side on the outside and two on each side on the inside, so it took me a good five minutes to go through everything. I found my GPS, mobile phone, camera, tracking device, satellite phone, iPod, wet wipes, batteries and toothpaste. I also carried a bum bag, where my horizontal hydration system lived, along with an enticing collection of sweet and savoury snacks. I had to ensure that if something happened, I'd have easily accessible extra layers, so I pulled out my down jacket and wrapped it firmly around my waist. I was now content that if I did fall and lose the Polar Cycle, I'd be able to survive for some time on these supplies.

Now firmly attached to the Polar Cycle and still in my lowest gear, I began pedalling. The ground had levelled out, but after five minutes, I stopped again to rearrange my kit, causing me to heel in the opposite direction. I had no idea if I was on the traverse. The snow beneath me was soft, and the unbalanced weight meant that the right front wheel was digging in so much that it was causing the rear wheel to spin. I was not moving anywhere.

I wanted to continue my pedalling battle but forced myself to stop to rearrange the weight in my panniers as the Polar Cycle rocked unnervingly from side to side. I pulled out five days of food rations that I'd added to the right-hand pannier bag and put it back into the pannier on the left, where it originally belonged. In total, this weighed about seven kilos, and it helped immediately with the balance of the Polar Cycle. I continued to pedal.

With visibility down to almost nothing, I sensed I was back on the traverse but my difficulties were far from over. I had to lean over to the right of my seat and hang my upper body behind the front wheel as much as possible because the right front wheel threatened to lift off the ice. My heart missed a beat at every pedal turn as I desperately fought to reconnect the right wheel with the ice. I tried to calm myself by counting the pedal strokes as a form of meditation.

61 pedal strokes later, and the gradient seemed to level out. My GPS was telling me to head further to the right, and as I did so, the traverse fell away, and I was confronted with my first very steep climb. During my practice visit to the glacier in Iceland, I found I couldn't cycle up

anything when the snow conditions were soft. Even the twelve per cent gradient at the ski slope in Tamworth had been a torturous workout. This was far worse.

I needed to counter my negative feelings with a surge of energy. Eagerly, my hand rummaged through my bum bag. I consumed a concoction of chocolate, biltong, and jellybeans; their flavours tinged with the saltiness of the pretzels jumbled within my eclectic energy mix.

Visibility was gradually improving, and I could now see about ten metres ahead of me. I wasn't sure if I was prepared for this extra information. The previous lack of visibility had comforted me—a security shield I could not see through. There was little wind and an almost eerie silence all around. "I am so lucky that there is no wind. Please, please, please stay this way," I begged. As I gazed ahead, I could see the beginning of the first 'over 20 per cent' gradient section, and I had run out of gears. I had used my lowest gear all morning, and no more options existed. In desperation, I stuffed a strand of liquorice in my mouth whilst still trying to digest the biltong combo that had by now lodged itself in between my teeth.

From that moment on, I went into a trance, totally absorbed in my chewing. I discovered great pleasure in trying to release food items lodged between my teeth with only my tongue. I'd always had a pet hate for people who tried to suck food out of their teeth in public but being on my own in the middle of Antarctica, it was all strangely comforting, and I certainly wasn't offending anyone.

Sometimes, I managed it easily. On other occasions, it took me up to two hours to dislodge the offending item. I needed this diversion to settle my mind because now was not the time to lose control. I was cycling through the Transantarctic Mountain Range alone, in my last gear, in poor visibility on a 25% gradient.

As my game faded, I was promptly transported back into the world of pain. My knee began to spasm; my back was very sore; my thighs felt like they were being ripped by every pedal rotation, and my breathing was heavy. "Slow is fine," I said to myself as I began the next pedal turn.

The slope of the earlier traverse had accumulated a fair amount of wind-blown snow, which caused some traction problems, but as I turned to the right to realign myself with my GPS reading, it seemed that the overnight winds had blown much of the snow drift away and I was left with a nicely compacted section of snow and ice. I prayed the studs in my rear tyres would help my traction. I hoped also that the effort that went into putting them into my tyres would be worth it. The incline began to increase, and at the same time, the mist started to lift. I could now see the top of this section of the climb. As far as I could judge, I had about a hundred metres to go.

Suddenly, the Polar Cycle struggled to move forward, and I needed to use my hands on the front wheels. My thighs were giving up. With all my might, I pushed with one pedal and pulled with the other. My heart beat fast, and the sweat began to run down my cheeks into my face mask. I knew I was in dangerous territory. I could not let myself sweat because if I reached the Polar Plateau covered in sweat and the temperature dropped to minus 40 degrees Celsius, I would freeze to death. I now had more than just climbing the glacier to worry about.

I pushed harder with my legs and less with my upper body, which helped control my heart rate and my sweat rate. The twinges in my right knee through over-exertion grew ever stronger. The repetitive thought of falling off the Polar Cycle and losing it down the glacier hit me in the heart, and I let out a painful cry. It was so steep I could not take the pressure off my legs. I had to keep the Polar Cycle moving and nudged it slowly, inch by inch, in an upward direction. My thighs must not fail me now.

The ever-growing pain in my right knee worried me as I was in the early days of my journey. I worked hard at controlling my breathing and only allowed myself to look ahead two metres at a time. I was moving at less than 0.2 kilometres per hour. I refused to allow myself to stop because the extra exertion of getting started again on such an incline would prove even harder. Instead, I began counting my pedal revolutions again.

I stared desperately at the logo on the inside wheel rim that crawled around slowly like a water wheel during a drought, counting each revolution in my head. At one point, it took twelve seconds for a revolution. I looked left and right and desperately tried to think of something to help my legs continue their work. I felt desperate and alone. I knew I was out of options. I breathed in deeply and forced my body to relax in the seat. I reminded myself that I had chosen to do this and that pain was temporary. I swore at the harness giving me completely avoidable pain. The incline was far more challenging than I had imagined, and I was only halfway up the glacier.

# 15. Tougher Than Expected

"When the pain seems too much to bear,
I imagine it being twice as bad"

The rest of the climb was a complete blur. Hour after hour yielded very little progress, and following my GPS in whiteout conditions with only two metres of visibility was torturous, as it only confirmed the lack of distance I had covered. After nine hours of virtually non-stop cycling, I was devastated to discover I'd only made twelve kilometres.

My rest stops during the day were dictated by when and where I could stop safely. At times, bracing my legs in a neutral position was the only way to prevent the Polar Cycle from rolling backwards. I jammed on the hand brake, but I could feel it straining to hold as I inched backwards until I built up the strength in my legs to push through a part revolution to bring me back to a stationary position.

I operated in a strange, remote sort of way, as though my body was somehow detached from my mind, but amazingly, I kept going. My watch told me I was now at 2850 metres and very near the top of the glacier. There seemed to be no clear top to this mountain range. Instead, it stretched away in an endless, blinding snow sheet. Since starting my journey, I had covered 108 kilometres.

After a few more leg-wrenching pushes with my thighs, I finally reached the top of the glacier and saw the Polar Plateau extending before me. It was featureless, empty and daunting. Here, I really understood the true meaning of biting cold. The crystal-clear blue sky began to cloud over, and the wind gathered momentum at an alarming rate. The wind howled and blew endless blizzards of stinging ice crystals around my lonely form. Antarctica was revealing its harsh side, and I was experiencing a real storm. It felt like I had stepped into another world, and I considered retracing my track a few hundred metres to take shelter on the glacier.

On the Polar Plateau, the wind blows in one direction, away from the South Pole, so I was facing it head-on. I gazed ahead and saw intermittent breaks in the cloud from the direction of the prevailing wind. Remaining focused, I pushed on southward. Despite my face being fully shielded by a mask, I found myself angling my head away to prevent the piercing chill and sharp snow granules from breaching its protection. The freezing air hit the back of my throat, and deep inside my lungs, I could feel a stabbing pain as the penetrating cold invaded my whole body.

I increased my cycling pace and temporarily put my knee pain to the back of my mind. As soon as I broke the routine of about 50 revolutions per minute, the pain returned with a vengeance.

After a while, the snow drifts reduced, and a steady wind blew the surface snow directly towards my tyres, which gave me the sensation that I was travelling at a far greater speed than I really was. It was the same scenario as paddling a boat against the tidal flow. This helped with morale and enabled me to focus on something other than the throbbing of my right knee. I must have been somewhat delusional because I was convinced I was going downhill. Yet there was only one way to the Pole: due south uphill!

I didn't want to camp just yet because I needed to be sure I was well away from the top ridge of the glacier. After a few more kilometres, I was too exhausted to continue. The snow was soft and deep, and as I rolled off the Polar Cycle with relief, I lay momentarily in the snow. For a split second, it felt soft and comforting. It didn't last. The biting cold wind picked me up off my back in a matter of seconds and refocused my attention back to tent building.

It was my first camping experience on the Polar Plateau, and I knew I needed to layer plenty of snow onto the valances of my tent. It was strange to call it night-time because the sun was still up; it never disappeared but circled around me. People in Antarctica live in many different time zones, and one person's night is another person's day, and the only two places on Earth where international date lines meet are at the actual South and North Poles.

When it came to camping time, I reminded myself of how much more difficult it had been to erect my tent in the dark, as I had often done on Lake Baikal, uncertain of the dangers around me. At least now I had light on my side. Nevertheless, I struggled impatiently as I removed two layers of gloves for the required seconds to fight with the poles and erect my tent. Two layers were essential to protect against the Polar Plateau's lower temperatures.

I didn't remove my base layer gloves for the remainder of the expedition, and they became a second skin. I decided not to look at them too closely because, by now, they were covered in all sorts of edible and non-edible items from my snack bag.

Paradoxically, every job required a mixture of patience and speed. If I touched metal, such as the Polar Cycle or the tent poles, the time I could keep my hands out of the mittens, with only the base layer gloves on, was less than if I was handling the tent fabric or a pannier bag. Work on anything metal was limited to a ten-second stint, after which time I hurriedly pulled the mittens back on, praying that my blood circulation would improve and warm up my fingers. To keep up the momentum, I swung my arms around wildly in a windmill fashion to urge the blood down to my numbed fingertips.

As I worked, out of the corner of my eyes, I caught sight of a bright light in the distance that flickered and faded like a comet flying through the skies. I gazed for a moment before the chill returned to my body, and I was reminded harshly that anything familiar was just an illusion. "Antarctica is beautiful but vicious," I repeated to myself.

The next day on the Polar Plateau was my most challenging, though I had feared the Leverett Glacier would be the hardest part of my journey. Conditions on the Ross Ice Shelf and the Leverett Glacier had been favourable, with a firm compacted surface, but now my progress was hampered. Mounds of snow appeared more frequently, and it wasn't long before the whole surface was covered in a thick layer of deep, soft snow. My worst fear became a reality. I struggled hour after hour, barely making any progress and fighting the increasing pain in my knee and uncertainty in my head. I desperately needed a plan.

If I continued at this meagre speed for the rest of the journey, I would miss the deadline at the Pole in time to catch the trucks before they began to travel back to Union Glacier for over-wintering. My debts for the expedition would spiral. The thought of the truck having to pick me up and drive me the last 100 kilometres so that they could meet this deadline was heartbreaking. The trucks were my only lifeline to the airbase, which lay 1,000 miles from the Pole in order for me to fly home.

I had twenty days to complete this journey and was already five days into it. Fifteen days at my current speeds of between two and three kilometres per hour was not very promising at all. My brain was buzzing with calculations, desperately trying to find an answer. The harsh fact was that the answer always remained the same. If I couldn't increase my pace, I would miss the deadline. I panicked and once again burst into a flood of tears that instantly froze, making my face mask very uncomfortable. It was wet on the inside and iced up on the outside. Every time I tried to answer the problem, my panic rose uncontrollably. I forced myself to keep the pedals turning. Every revolution of the pedal was one revolution less, I told myself.

I had already calculated in my head that the approximate number of revolutions it would take to cycle to the South Pole was 640,000, and based on where I was now, I had 521,542 revolutions to go. I began counting backwards, chanting 521,541 left to go, 521,540 left to go, 521,539 left to go… Despite such insignificant progress, this helped my morale and allowed me to manage my fears. It also helped me pass the time as I stumbled over the long numbers.

To add to my discomfort, the chain had begun to squeak noisily. I had chosen not to use any form of lubrication as this was the right choice on Lake Baikal. As I wondered how to solve the squeak, I began to choke on the piece of biltong I'd been chewing for the past hour. A resolution to the annoying squeak came into my mind. "Well, yes, why not give it a go," I thought. At my next rest stop, I rubbed biltong on my chain vigorously. It did the trick and stopped the squeak instantly. "How's that for resourcefulness!" I said to myself.

The going was steep, soft and strenuous, and after 13 hours, I was exhausted. It was time to stop for food and sleep. Suddenly, in the whiteness, I could see a darkened blob that looked like strangely shaped rocks perched on the surface of the snow. I squinted and scanned the horizon again. As I cycled closer, I saw it was a fuel drop from the South Pole traverse.

This became my target for the day. During the final few kilometres, I humorously wondered whether this 'service station' might have a Costa Coffee or Starbucks! I envisioned the comforting heat of the dark, fragrant coffee as it slipped down my throat, infused with a sense of comfort and warmth, paired with a rocky road, my preferred treat. But there was no coffee shop; the fuel drop comprised a stack of 20-30 barrels, which would provide fuel for the vehicles returning along the South Pole. They looked dramatic and uncanny, as though they had been abandoned carelessly in this pristine environment. I pedalled on just one extra kilometre because I knew that anything I could do today would be less to do tomorrow. I was saddened by the fact that I was desperately looking forward to the expedition being over because it was now not only a race against time and the other cyclists, but I was also battling with serious injury.

I erected my tent quickly and gratefully slumped into it. I had a plan before I got too comfortable, or rather less uncomfortable than I had been, during yet another day of sheer physical and mental exhaustion. I was still travelling with ice studs in my rear tyres, which I had relied heavily on while climbing the glacier, but now they were a hindrance. The snow and ice were sticking to them, and as my wheels revolved, they collected huge chunks of snow, making cycling much more difficult. These studs had taken hours to put in. Now, I needed to start the unenviable task of trying to remove them.

I scrambled through my tool bag, which, apart from using the pump the day before, had yet to see much use. I found the tool for extracting the studs. Removing the studs had to be accomplished with multiple layers of gloves on because taking them off would undoubtedly lead to frost-bitten figures. There were 120 studs across the three tyres that had to be removed. I placed the tool on the top of the first ice stud, leaned with my weight onto the screw and tried turning it in an anti-clockwise direction. It didn't move an inch. I tried again, and the tool slipped off the head of the screw. On the third attempt, my focus and sheer determination produced a result, and the ice stud popped out and fell into the snow. I grabbed the small plastic bag containing spare ice studs, scooped up the one lying in the snow, and placed it in the bag. Even this tiny screw made the Antarctica landscape look littered. My counting game began again as I counted down the screws I was removing. Hindered by my bulky gloves, coupled with frozen hands and lack of mental concentration, I rarely succeeded on the first attempt to remove each screw. I became angry and yawned at the same time. Three hours later, I was combining ice stud removal with my whole tent routine. The effort was debilitating, but at least I could congratulate myself on my ability to multi-task on a whole new scale.

Clumsily spooning mushroom soup into my mouth like a messy toddler, I used my Spork, which was haphazardly fixed with gaffer tape, resulting in an awkward utensil that fell short of its intended function.

I had to plunge my hand deep into the food packet to scrape up the contents, covering my hand and knuckles with greasy mushroom soup. I licked them clean between each plunge, knowing I was consuming 600 calories of much-needed energy.

This multi-tasking, however, was short-lived as I experienced a culinary disaster. While I handled my main meal food pouch with great care, hydrating it in my sleeping bag to make the most of its warmth, I managed to damage the seam on the zip-locked food pouch as I opened it. Inevitably, chaos followed. I tipped the pouch over and covered my sleeping bag in spaghetti Bolognese. I tried to mop up the disaster with my limited wet wipes, but they were not enough to remove the evidence. From now on, I knew I'd have to endure this sickly smell of spaghetti Bolognese every day. It added to my building discomfort.

With less oxygen in the air and the effects of mild altitude sickness returning, I had to force myself to eat. I didn't care anymore about the subtleties of food, of which there was little in my freeze-dried rations; all I wanted was energy to fuel and protein to repair my body. I adopted the technique of holding my nose to reduce the taste and smell. After hours of sheer physical fatigue, my body was not taking kindly to being topped up with three thousand calories of food in one hour.

After eating, I was still sitting part in and part out of the tent with my rear wheel in between my legs to assist with removing the ice studs. My feet felt numb, and my legs were aching from the awkward position I had forced them into. I had removed well over half of the studs, and I needed desperately to sleep and rest my throbbing knee, which had now swollen up to such a size that my trousers stretched uncomfortably around it.

I had no idea whether my injured kneecap was still in place or if the swelling had swamped it. I tugged nervously at the braces on my trousers, holding my breath, but they were difficult to remove in such a confined space. I tugged off the over trousers with haste and immediately felt a sense of relief. Despite being designed to allow for bending my knee, the feeling of crumbled fabric at the back of my knee was finally removed. I stretched out my legs awkwardly, rubbing my hand up and down my thighs.

At first, everything seemed okay, but it was much more swollen than yesterday. I paused before taking off my thermal layer, giving my lower body a moment to air. I reasoned that if I couldn't see the damage I was causing my body, it might be easier to push through the bad times. If I knew my kneecap had shifted or my knee had turned blue and swollen, then the thought may hinder my progress. My attention turned temporarily to the sore on my back from the earlier use of the harness on the glacier. I also had a frostbitten left cheek, and after removing two layers of socks, my toes looked deathly white. I told myself that I was in control while I was in my tent. I must deal with my kaleidoscope of injuries one by one.

I had to strain to reach down to rub my toes, one foot at a time, generating heat through friction since I couldn't bend my right knee. Luckily, my flexibility and long arms allowed for this yogic manoeuvre. I placed the hydration system underneath my feet, which I had just filled with hot water, and the heat gradually radiated into my frozen toes. Wrapping up my feet in my sleeping bag, I began to feel them again. My first problem was solved. The next job was to remove my thermal trousers without disturbing my feet. I lay back on my sleeping bag and slowly peeled the layer from my body with my thumbs tucked into the waistband. I lifted my bottom to pull them down to my knees, but as I did so, my knee yelled in pain, and I collapsed back down in a heap.

There was no time to feel sorry for myself. I sat up and hurriedly rolled the thermals down to my ankles. My right knee was huge because the kneecap had been drowned in synovial fluid to protect it from the relentless turn of the pedal.

During my many mathematical calculations, I worked out that I had bent this knee 42,000 times based on my distance today. I reached for my first aid kit, sitting in the orange dry bag beside my electrical department. I took out the arnica gel and, at the same time, placed my toothbrush, which had fallen out of the bag, into my mouth to avoid misplacing it.

Despite being very sore, I kneaded my knuckles fiercely into my thighs in an attempt to relieve the knots and free some of the lactic acid that was making them feel tighter by the day. I applied a generous amount of gel onto my right knee and gently massaged it with my right hand, using a circular motion. As I did so, I felt what I believed to be the synovial fluid being pushed around the kneecap. I had no idea whether this pummelling was going to help me get through the trauma. From my knowledge and experience, I knew the only solution for repairing repetitive strain injuries was rest, but that was a luxury I couldn't afford. I couldn't risk taking time out to wait for my knee to recover for fear that bad weather may strike and my dream of reaching the South Pole in time would be over.

The gel had now been absorbed, and after a further five minutes of frantic thigh massage, I was exhausted. I took a quick look at my toes, which were now in a far happier state. I removed the hydration system and placed it beside my head. My aches and pains were relieved only slightly as I drifted into the arms of a restless slumber.

# 16. Progress but Not as Planned

"Learn from your choices and never regret them"

That night, I slept fitfully due to the throbbing in my knee that kept me awake; even the simple task of turning onto my side caused shooting pain. The big dilemma ahead was that I had over 300 kilometres left to go on the Polar Plateau, and if snow conditions stayed the same, I might miss my deadline at the Pole.

The following day, the mounds of snow built up even higher than before, and I constantly sank into the snow with all my wheels. The rear wheel was sinking even deeper due to the weight of the kit on my back. I swore about the fact that I was stupidly trying to cycle three wheels through soft snowdrifts. With one less wheel, it would be two-thirds less drag as the two wheels would follow in a single track. I was creating three tracks. At least I didn't have to stop and get off the Polar Cycle all the time and push through the drifts, which I would have had to do on a two-wheeled bike. I thought constantly about how things would have been different if I'd opted for a fat bike but came to the same conclusion. With a fat bike, there was no way I would have managed to cycle the whole way up the Leverett Glacier, nor would I have been able to cycle in this deep snow that I was now driving myself through stubbornly.

On a fat bike, I would have to dismount every few pedal rotations to lift the front wheel out of a deep drift. I would also be going at a similar painfully slow speed. The only option with a fat bike would have been to push it and walk alongside. I was relieved by this repetitive reasoning and credited my team and me for coming up with a superior cycle solution, even though further improvements could have been made if time had permitted. Having two or even three-wheel drive could have made the difference. Now, I had to settle for the fact that I only had a rear-wheel-driven cycle.

I chewed on a piece of biltong and wondered how long it would take to feel my energy levels rise. Would I be able to raise the levels sufficiently to get me through this? I really needed more power in my thighs. Stopping for a brief interlude, I swigged hot coffee from the flask in my pannier and climbed back on the Polar Cycle.

I had already achieved something that no one else had before. I had pedalled every metre of the Leverett Glacier and a fair chunk of the Polar Plateau. I now had to focus on maintaining this for the rest of the journey.

I pedalled on stubbornly, now at a speed that was so slow it barely registered on my GPS. After an hour or so, I gazed back for the first time and still had a clear sight of the fuel drums. I had barely made any distance at all. The harsh reality of my situation began to unnerve me. I sighed, sigh after sigh, trying to figure out my options. I needed to prepare for the worst. I could only estimate the distance ahead based on my current speed, which was appallingly slow. Even without bad weather days in the equation, I'd need a further 15 days to reach my goal, which would put me right on the limit. I had to consider the looming possibility that I would not make it on time.

I was in pain and felt a deep sadness. I had successfully tackled the most challenging part of the expedition, yet massive difficulties and time constraints lay ahead. The biting cold was searing my soul and hindered my every move. My knee was very painful, and this bloody deep snow was becoming ridiculous.

My pace had slowed so much that I longed for skis during a blip in my focus. "What was I doing? Why was I doing this? Cycling in snow is not a sport, nor is it fun. It's ridiculous! No wonder every sensible person chooses to ski to the Pole. Why did I not have a pair of skis on my feet? Skis would make this going easy. They would glide over the deep, soft snow, and they wouldn't sink," I thought.

I had to remind myself that skiing had no role in this expedition. I was out to prove that what seemed impossible was possible, and where others had failed, I was determined to succeed. I also realised that if I had had a sledge for this section of the expedition, I would have been able to drag my kit, allowing the Polar Cycle to float over the soft snow—but it was a luxury I did not have.

With angry determination, I persisted in forcing my tired legs to turn the pedals. Three pedal rotations counted for just under one full revolution of the wheels. I was totally out of breath, and fireworks were sparking from my right knee. I was not going to make it. I sat with my hands cupping my face and elbows resting on my thighs.

I took a brief rest stop to try to work out a plan, but it only turned me into a trembling body of frustration. Swear words tumbled from my lips. I had two choices. Either I continued stubbornly at this slow and painful pace, or I'd have to work out how to stop the Polar Cycle from sinking into the snow and increase my speed. Reducing the weight I was carrying on the back of the Polar Cycle would almost certainly help, but would it be enough?

I was angry that I would have to deviate from my original plan of completing the journey unsupported. I wrestled with my mind, my painful body and all the expectations I had saddled myself with. I hadn't yet failed, but it felt like failure. I thought briefly about my competitors who had resorted to walking, skiing and receiving support with food drops. I looked at my heavy kit bags and instantly made a decision.

The 55 kilograms of kit I'd started off with still amounted to around 50 kilograms and enough to make me question for the first time how different it would be to cycle without the weight. It was time to experiment. I threw my panniers to the ground and cycled twenty metres on—it was as though a huge weight had been lifted off my shoulders, which it had. The simple fact of having less weight on the rear of the Polar Cycle was enough to give me the ability to float much better on top of the deep snow. It wasn't all plain sailing because, at times, I still sank, but removing the weight and less pressure on my knee made me realise that this was a new possibility; I just needed to adapt my plan.

It was an emotional twenty minutes as I dragged my kit back to the Polar Cycle, trying to figure out what this would mean for the expedition. Until now, I had been unsupported, carrying all my kit and fending for myself entirely. At the beginning of the expedition, I had asked Emil, Torfi, and Wayne not to interfere and to keep a good distance away from me. They stuck to their word, but as I cycled those twenty metres without my panniers, I realised this was the only solution to reaching the Pole in good time.

I fought off the demon telling me that this was a failure and told myself that all good plans are adapted to suit the environment and situation. I certainly had an environmental challenge on my hands. This

139

adjustment to the plan and technically becoming a supported expedition due to the trucks carrying some of my kit would change the dynamics of my mission. I gazed at my GPS and reaffirmed the distance ahead. With an increase in speed of two kilometres per hour, which I was confident I could gain, it would take me 13 days to the Pole. This, however, was still too close for comfort as I had not allowed for bad weather.

I needed to remove some weight. It was now the only option. I didn't have the benefit of hindsight, so I had to plan for the conditions to stay as they were. I recalled the truck journey to the start point and the large sastrugi field that lay ahead. Things were about to get even worse. I reorganised one pannier and left the two heaviest ones, which accounted for about 35 kilograms of weight, on the snow. With much reluctance but a complete understanding that this was the lifeline to a successful outcome, I radioed Emil. There was no response. I could only assume that he could hear me, but I couldn't hear him. I continued to give him my GPS position and said I'd left some kit on the ice and could he please collect it.

I knew that he would be following my tracks and, given that we had both recorded the route on the downward journey onto our GPS, our tracks would be the same, give or take a few metres. A large pile of kit lying on the Antarctic landscape could be seen for miles, and he would not miss it. I thought no more and pedalled off at an accelerated speed.

I didn't allow myself to think about what I'd done for the next hour. Any feeling of regret at this stage would tear my dreams apart. I am a very conscientious person who is always trying to do the right and best thing, so having to make a change of plan in my mind was devastating. I couldn't allow this self-punishment to happen just yet. With no emotion, I cycled on, keeping thoughts to a minimum and only focusing on the goal of arriving at the South Pole in good time.

Like most other expeditions that have food drops, I was now receiving the same support because I was no longer carrying everything I needed. The feelings of regret crept back intermittently, and I felt angry. I constantly recalculated my speed and returned to the same conclusion; even if I had managed to put in 20 hours per day, I would not have made the progress needed at the speed I was going.

Feeling my tyres floating more freely over the snow was a great relief. I needed to bottle this sense of freedom of movement as I knew I'd need it later in the expedition as my knee weakened by the hour.

A little while later, I could hear the roar of the trucks approaching, and they pulled up alongside me. After speaking with Wayne and Emil,

I could see how Antarctica was also being harsh to them. With his beard longer than I'd ever seen, Wayne was wearing every item of clothing he had packed. He was sombre and silent, and I felt instantly responsible for putting him through this scenario. Seeing his eyes appearing from behind his face mask, lacking their usual sparkle, and his frustration with endless putting on and taking off clothing as he stepped from inside to outside the truck riddled me with guilt. He never wanted to be here in the first place, but he still supported me, and for that, I was eternally grateful.

Emil and Wayne stepped out of the truck and approached me, gazing down at what must have been a very sorry sight. I sat in a slightly slumped position, awaiting their comments. Emil was patient and calming, but after almost two months of sitting in the driving seat of his truck, I could see he longed for home. His long beard was now even longer, and a few strands of straggly hair had appeared on his otherwise bald head. He wore all black and seemed to have fewer clothes than anyone else.

I had so enjoyed my time on my own, making my own decisions, but I was now responsible for drawing them further into my expedition. "Good decision," Wayne said. I perked up.

"We followed your tyre tracks and could see how deep they were, and we were beginning to discuss your chances of success," Emil said.

"I know you've got strong legs; we could see how hard going it must have been, but now you have a better chance of succeeding," Wayne added.

I knew they were both making these comments for my own good, but I could also tell they were relieved that this would mean they would get home earlier. "From now on, I must cover good ground each day to not disappoint them," I told myself.

From a human-powered perspective, expeditioners travel between 10-40 kilometres per day in Antarctica. Until now, I had managed 14 kilometres on my worst day, travelling up the Leverett Glacier and just short of 50 kilometres on my best day. Now I felt responsible for getting everyone home in good time, so I decided to cycle at least 50 kilometres every day, whatever was going on and how much my knee hurt. The only thing that could stop me now was bad weather.

Somehow, my knee would just have to work with me. My mind was gaining strength and taking over my body's weakness. With the weight removed and a new dynamic to my expedition, it was now all about speed and ensuring I was the first person to cycle the whole way to the South Pole.

I cycled with the freedom and feeling of weightlessness. I still had a 20-kilogram Polar Cycle and 60-kilogram body to move through the snow, but after cycling part way across the Ross Ice Shelf, up the 3,000 metres Leverett Glacier and a short distance on the Polar Plateau with my full load on board, this felt like luxury. I just had to manage my crippling knee pain. The temperature began to dip more each day, and for the first time on the expedition, I thought, yes, I can do this. It was December 23, the seventh day of the expedition; the Transantarctic Mountain range had slid out of view, and all that was left was the vast, barren Polar Plateau. Now, with a plan that was working well, I just needed to balance my self-punishment of 50 kilometres a day against my fatiguing body. It was a constant battle, and my attention turned to home with Christmas Eve fast approaching.

It was the first time in my 35 years that I had not been with my family for Christmas. We follow the Swedish tradition of celebrating Christmas on Christmas Eve, and then, to the envy of our friends, we also had a second Christmas on Christmas Day. My mother, sister, and I had always worked together as a great team, and I usually found myself preparing the herring salad and decorating the gingerbread house, as my mother focused on preparing the ham and the spare ribs, whilst my sister polished the brass and decorated the table. The Swedish flag took prime position in the centre of the table, as did the many candles spread around the kitchen and living room. The whole evening was candlelit, and with my sister's young children running around the house, I relived my special childhood memories.

The gentle aroma of Christmas permeated the house with a combination of gingerbread, boiled ham, and warm glögg that my father had prepared on the hob. The sound of our Swedish Christmas music, which accompanied us on the traditional long dance, echoed in my mind. With my father leading the way, we swung around the kitchen and sitting room, dancing and singing our hearts out. Our Swedish Christmas at home in Wales was about to begin, and I wasn't there.

These memories made me pine for home. I missed everyone and was hit by a wave of guilt not only because of the discomfort that Wayne was putting up with. I knew my family would have an unsettled Christmas, fearing for my safety, as I pedalled away on a massive ice cap at the bottom of the world. What was I doing? Why break up such a wonderful tradition? I just wanted to be back home. I adored my parents, sister, and her children; they were all my best friends. God, how I missed them!

After a full day of cycling, Emil pulled up alongside me and asked when I was planning to stop for a sleep. I hadn't really thought about it because I was now obsessed with kilometres. My GPS recorded that I had covered over seventy kilometres on this day—much better than I had expected. The reduced weight on the Polar Cycle profoundly affected my cycling ability, and the compacted snow conditions also seemed to be on my side. I still faced large snow drifts but could maintain a good speed if I cycled around them. I cycled on with a degree of excited anticipation.

For some reason, the next two kilometres were a real struggle. My knee was exploding with pain, and my muscles were screaming. Why the change, I thought?

Until now, I'd been very much in my own world, but now I had to deal with other people's comments and opinions. Were they trying to tell me it was time to stop?

"My knee is killing me, but I don't want to stop", I mumbled through my face mask. Even though I had maintained good speeds during the day, it was my painful knee rather than the snow conditions I had been battling.

"I want to try and reach eighty kilometres today, I'm ten kilometres away from that," I continued. "I can't bear to look at my GPS any longer as the kilometres are going by so slowly. Can you overtake me every three kilometres and then stop so I have an indication of the distance I've cycled? I think that will help me," I admitted stubbornly.

Emil sensed my anxiety but, as always, remained calm and did exactly as I asked. The roar of the truck behind me every 30 minutes gave me renewed strength. Finally, I mastered the last few kilometres.

Wayne and Torfi joined us at 82 kilometres and quickly erected the overnight camp. As we climbed into our tents, I could see Wayne's frustration as the biting cold was gnawing at him. Was this a test too far for our relationship?

# 17. Christmas on the Polar Plateau

"There is no one right path to follow"

Now, on the seventh night of my expedition, Wayne was in a grumpy mood. His fingers had been frozen badly from wearing thin gloves whilst taking photos and putting up his tent night after night. I would be indebted to him for the rest of my life for putting him through such an ordeal. Not only was he freezing cold, but he was also bored out of his mind from sitting in a truck, day after day, with nothing to do.

He seemed to be worrying about his businesses he'd been forced to neglect over the last month. To add to the worries, we bought a new house in August that was now well underway with renovation work. What if the builders do something drastically wrong, he questioned? We barely spoke to each other that evening and kept our distance as I had, once again, to maintain my strength to finish what I had set myself to do. It was a different expedition from the one I started, but the result, hopefully, would be the same – a world-first title was in sight.

Was my goal more important than my relationship, I pondered? If I jumped into the truck, we could be back at the South Pole in about six hours and the pain would stop for everyone. It was an action I could not take. I reasoned that if our relationship was supposed to be, then it should survive anything, even something as extreme as this. I longed for the day when Wayne, with a smile on his face, would turn round and say:" It was a fabulous experience." I desperately wanted him to understand my 'type two fun'—agony at the time, but a great sense of relief when it is all over. However, I had to admit that to most people, I probably had a masochistic sense of fun!

I hoped Wayne's personal achievement would be experiencing the most incredible place on Earth and seeing his partner achieve her lifelong dream. Was I just being selfish again? Wayne was highly successful in business. He had created the best off-road running and fitness shoes, now selling in 60 countries, and built up a brilliant team that all seemed to love working for INOV8. As any boss will know, it's tough to balance business, finances and team welfare, but he had it nailed. Work was his passion, and I wanted to reciprocate his support for my expedition.

I barely closed my eyes that night, and by 5 a.m. on day eight, I was already up, dressed, and hobbling in the vague direction of the Polar Cycle. It lay tightly secured to the truck only eight metres away, yet that journey was one of emotion, pain, suffering, and total numbness. The only way I could force myself to start cycling was not to think. I had to blank out everything to gather enough courage to begin my day.

As I cycled in the cold, cut off from my friends and family, there were many reasons to stop cycling and only one reason to keep going. That one reason was so immense that it, without question, overpowered any reasons to stop.

Antarctica had taken over my mind. It was my new companion: pure, white, unpredictable, exciting. Strangely, its danger strengthened me and taught me how to suffer and fight on. I contemplated my hunger for adventure. Did its roots lie in the fact that my older sister had always spurred me on to go first and see what was around the next corner? Or was it due to my overriding compulsion to do the opposite of what people expected of me, like studying maths when everyone had told me I was not good enough? Or was it thanks to my parents, who always believed in stepping through the open door? Undoubtedly, it was a combination of all these things.

Christmas Eve in the freezing snow felt uninspiring, and the 'Happy Christmas' exchange of words with Wayne, Emil, and Torfi melted into the whiteness. In Sweden and Iceland, it is tradition to celebrate Christmas on Christmas Eve. With sadness, I felt that I wasn't the only one reminiscing. All three were missing their families back home because of my expedition. Emil talked passionately about his two daughters; I could tell he was a dedicated and loving father. I forced myself to chase away the sadness and concentrate on the task at hand.

My speed on the Polar Plateau became even more urgent as my feet were freezing in addition to the incessant knee pain. I just couldn't keep them warm. The frost nip on my right foot, which I had suffered during the Patagonian race, had returned to haunt me. What a Christmas present, I thought. Would I come home with all my toes intact, I wondered? When my feet felt cold, I was relatively relaxed, but then came the worrying sensation of heat, followed by total numbness. This was serious, so I stopped every 30 minutes and performed ten high-energy jumps. As my boots landed with a thump on the snow, I got the blood pumping again, allowing me to cycle for a further few kilometres. The problem was it only aggravated my knee pain.

On top of this, I had begun to develop frost nip on my right cheek, which I had spotted the night before whilst giving myself the once over. There had been a gap between my goggles and my face mask, which the freezing air had penetrated. This began to bother me, and although it wasn't causing me any pain at this stage, it was another thing on my mind. I hoped that it would not cause permanent damage to my cheek, as inevitably, that would be something I'd have to live with for the rest of my life. I became obsessed with ensuring my cheek was covered by tucking my neoprene face mask under my goggles, causing them to steam up and hindering my sight and progress.

On occasions in my snowbound world, my Polar Cycle felt as though it was freewheeling. The combination of fatigue and my body being so programmed to cycle made me oddly detached. The angle of the horizon was my only reminder that I was still cycling uphill. I fell into a dream-like state: stillness, nothingness, emptiness, and silence, except for the overpowering crackling sound of my wheels through the snow. There was so much nothingness to take in—a haunting, empty canvas pressed down on me.

Emil was alone in his vehicle and was now staying closer to me. He drove a few kilometres behind because if I needed something from my kit bags, I could access them. As the days went on and my crippling knee pain continued, he came closer and closer to me during my breaks. If needed, I could hand him more things to carry by truck. He reciprocated with a gentle smile.

I was now cycling with only my bum bag around my waist containing my snacks and hydration system, my electrical equipment still stuffed down my bra and sleeping bag, which my head bounced against as I tried to rest on the move. Fully cocooned in my down clothing and with three layers of headwear muffling the sound, I was unaware of the truck behind me. I still made a point of not looking back. There was only one way; it was south and straight ahead.

The temperature was bitterly cold, and my body rapidly declined from over-exertion. I could feel the chill surrounding me, drawing my heat and dispersing it into the icy atmosphere. Whilst my body had been strong during the earlier stages of the expedition, and I could fight off the cold, a physical change had now occurred. I could no longer rely on exertion only to create the body heat I needed. In addition, I had to wear every item of clothing that belonged to me and pray it would be enough to ward off the freezing conditions.

I wondered how much more of the cold I could withstand. Was I nearing hypothermia or frostbite? Despite putting on all my clothes, the heat my body was creating and trapping between the layers was insufficient. I considered my home-grown theory of making myself a little colder by taking a layer off for a few seconds before putting it back on, hence tricking my body into feeling warmer. It was a gamble I could not take.

Instead, I tried to relax my busy mind to take advantage of the unique environment. I tried to fill it with the sheer beauty of nothingness and search for those special moments of uninterrupted contact with my spirit. I had no contact with Wayne and Torfi during the day, who travelled in the second vehicle; we were only reunited at the end of every painful day.

Even now, with the pain that throbbed through my body, I considered cycling a brilliant sport, and I also wanted my next expedition to be cycling-based. I considered how I could marry cycling with my second love of kayaking and pedalling on water and creating some pedal craft. Images of a pedalo with a swan's head flashed through my mind and made me giggle. The beginnings of yet another expedition metamorphosed in my mind.

Looking at my GPS, I noted that I had crossed the 88-degrees south latitude on the Polar Plateau. I had just under 220 kilometres to go, assuming the snow conditions allowed me to travel in a straight line. Up to this point, I had travelled 414 kilometres and was at a high altitude; my GPS flickered between 2,921 and 2,922 metres. However, staring at the numbers did little to lift my spirits. The pain in my knee was a harsh reminder that the remaining distance of over 200 kilometres was just too much.

My mind was populated by kilometres and how far one kilometre would take me. I broke my journey down into one-kilometre stretches. I then approximated 100 metres ten times by gazing up ahead and placing a fictitious dot on my horizon at the edge of a section of sastrugi, which twinkled in the bright sunlight.

After many days of strong wind on the Polar Plateau, much of the soft snow had been blown away, and the ice glistened in the sun. Tackling the sastrugi was a relief as it added some variety compared to the smooth, icy surface I'd been travelling on. The downside to the sastrugi was that they forced me to veer from my due-south heading, so the actual distance I was covering to the South Pole was far more than in a straight line. By doing this, I could avoid some of the steeper sections. I was amazed at how extreme the sastrugi had become, and in some areas, they rose steeply above the height of my head as I sat on the Polar Cycle and getting to the top required real technique.

As I approached a steep section of sastrugi, I had to increase the intensity of my pedalling enough to make it over the crest. The only thing that spurred me on was the knowledge that every up had a down. I felt I was on a fairground ride as I flew off the top at high speed. I had to move my weight around accurately and speedily to stay balanced on the Polar Cycle, but every drop from the top of the sastrugi produced three or four metres of freewheeling that gave my knee that all-important rest. There were many times that I failed to make it to the top. Instead, I rolled backwards at full speed with my legs spinning in reverse, adding to the throbbing pain in my knee.

While lying in my tent that evening, I pulled out my GPS to calculate my remaining distance to the Pole. There was a straight line of 157 kilometres left to my target. I had cycled 69 kilometres today—way down on my best day of 82 kilometres. I reasoned that if I could get back to 80 kilometres per day, then tomorrow, Christmas Day, would be my penultimate day, and I'd complete the expedition on December 26—in the most crazy, super fast time. Wow! The thought fired me up with excitement. However, with a whole morning of cycling over sastrugi to tackle, my speed was totally dependent on how my knee would hold out.

The next morning, with another high dosage of painkillers, I was up just after 5 am. There was no sign of wakefulness from anyone else, so I set off as soon as possible after treating myself to my usual porridge breakfast.

On the few occasions that Emil pulled up alongside me during the day, Wayne would stick his head out of the window and try to tell me how I should tackle the sastrugi. I felt like screaming at him. Pedalling as hard as I could, I reasoned that he was only trying to help me and offer some advice. He must have sensed my frustration at his comments because the next time Emil pulled up alongside, he was alone, and Wayne was now back in the second truck with Torfi.

After finally clearing the sastrugi field, the monotony of the Polar Plateau returned. There was little change on the horizon. My only diversion was my iPod. I mused at how dull the same 20 songs had become. Before the expedition, I hadn't had time to sort out my music collections, nor did I deem it important enough. Nevertheless, they accompanied me when I decided to sing at the top of my voice, sometimes in Swedish, sometimes in English, sometimes with a Welsh accent and sometimes with a hint of Jamaican!

Even my refreshments needed to be more varied. At regular intervals, my hand, still bearing its base layer glove, scurried around in my snack food bag lying around my waist. It had almost become a food item itself, embedded with chocolate and beef fat. I hoped I'd pull out a roast dinner or a pizza, but all I found were jellybeans, biltong and the occasional piece of liquorice covered in crumbed pretzels and broken chocolate. For some reason, the liquorice was almost frozen solid and took longer to chew than the biltong. Gentle chewing could take as long as 45 minutes for one three-inch strip of liquorice, which in distance time was 4.5 kilometres, so I devised a new measure of distance and called it "the chewometer."

My chewometer method helped me devour the kilometres as I chewed through the contents of my snack bag for most of the day. My jaws were aching by the end, and I dreaded my first visit to the dentist on my return. When analysing my distance, I was delighted that evening; I had managed 83 kilometres. I was truly flying. The conditions were perfect, but my body was nearing complete shutdown. The only thing that was pushing my pedals was the power of my mind.

I hadn't thought much about the other cyclists since reaching the Polar Plateau, but that evening, I asked Emil whether he'd heard any news. "You don't need to worry; they are still at 86 degrees; you're almost 300 kilometres ahead of them," he said.

I gasped with shock. I knew their route was further than mine, but I'd climbed a 3,000-metre-high glacier through the largest mountain range in Antarctica.

"They've really been struggling, and it looks like the Spaniard is mainly skiing now," continued Emil. "The American is quite a few days behind because he doesn't have skis and is walking a fair amount," Emil said. "His sledge also seems to be causing him problems."

I couldn't help but feel pleased with myself. My team and I had made some good choices. The route, the Polar Cycle and the timing for the expedition had all been favourable, and fortunately, despite some ferocious wind conditions, I was not forced to be tent-bound.

The only thing I now began to question was my decision to become supported. Gazing at my knee, I considered whether it would have coped with the additional 50 kilograms of weight. This was still very questionable. I might have been sitting here on my penultimate day, or I might not have been. It would have most certainly taken me much longer, maybe three times as long and then I'd be nearing the cut-off point. Looking up, I changed gear and refocused on what was now important. I needed to complete this expedition. For the first time, the end was in sight. I had covered 70 kilometres so far today, and only approximately 90 kilometres remained to the Pole.

Overnight, there was a ferocious storm, and as I lay tense inside my tent, I could hear the icy snow thumping on the canvas, threatening to rip it to threads. I lay with my eyes transfixed on the wildly flapping canvas roof, waiting for the worst to happen. Luckily, my tent held, but it was another night of intense sleep deprivation.

The next morning, day ten of the expedition, I climbed onto the Polar Cycle and dragged my right foot onto the pedal. Getting my foot firmly in place always took a few jerky movements. The pain from my swollen knee was excruciating. Would I have the strength for the last part of my journey? I breathed in deeply and began my first pedal rotation.

The shooting pain from my knee resounded in my head with a dull thumping, and hot flushes thundered across my forehead. I began to sweat. It felt as though my kneecap was being pulled from me. The pain was horrendous. Tears streamed down my face as I clutched my kneecap with my right hand, attempting to stabilise it. I had taken a handful of painkillers but was still waiting for them to take effect as I coaxed my reluctant legs into the familiar routine of spinning the pedals. Even when the painkillers worked, they only dampened the pain slightly, and any jerky movement dislodged my kneecap from its seat, and I'd gasp in pain.

The tears made my goggles steam up, causing me to swerve into the soft snow patches. The overnight storm had created snowdrifts everywhere, so the beginning of this day was particularly hard, and I had to use my hands to free my back wheel from the deep snow. At the same time, I had to work hard on pathfinding and choosing the optimum route. Although I was sick of the same songs by now, I sought solace in the best tracks on my iPod, "Loved Me Back to Life" by Celine Dion and "We Can't Stop" by Miley Cyrus. I had 72 kilometres ahead of me and was determined to make it today.

After a few hours, Emil crept up behind me. He had a lie-in that morning as he was preparing for a very long day. I'd already put in some 17-hour days, and I expect he was planning for an even longer day today. By now, he had learnt about my stubbornness and that failure was not an option. I had decided that today was the day I would become the first person in the world to cycle to the South Pole.

From the start, I'd been desperate to eat up the kilometres as fast as possible, but my priority changed by mid-morning. With less than 72 kilometres ahead of me, I realised that my lifelong dream might be over much sooner than expected. I'd been cycling for ten days, and suddenly, it all felt too short. This created an abundance of mixed feelings. I was desperate for my journey to be over, but at the same time, I was desperate for it not to be over. I cried because of the pain, and I cried because of the thought that this would be my last day. I was completely confused.

The temperature was just below minus 30 degrees Celsius, and my breath was freezing instantly on the outside of my face mask. My feet struggled for life, and my routine of stopping every half hour to exercise them became even more critical. I couldn't let some stupid mistake like frostbite be the cause of failure at this late stage.

Over the last few days, my appetite had diminished dramatically, which had something to do with the altitude and because my body had now readjusted to coping with long hours of extreme physical exertion. My overall energy levels were good, but I'd lost the taste for motivational food. A piece of liquorice or a chocolate bar was usually the highlight of my day, but both had lost their appeal. I was now just a machine operating on a minimal diet.

I began to think of my homebound journey and leaving behind the South Pole. I was excited about the prospect of finally climbing into a moving truck and being transported at a faster speed across the vast expanse of Antarctica. Our homebound journey would take us past the other two cyclists who were aiming for the title. I spared one last thought for them. They were still at 87 degrees south latitude and had over 300 kilometres to reach the South Pole, and I had just over 40 kilometres left to go. They were also travelling slower than I was, more like four kilometres per hour, whereas I was travelling at nine to ten kilometres per hour. If the conditions were good and I kept going, I would beat them to the Pole.

Had I only known what I know now, I would have battled on a little longer carrying my kit. The weather on the Polar Plateau had been relatively kind to me, and though I did not know it at the time, I would have probably made the deadline for flying out of Antarctica, knee-dependent, of course. For one last time, I beat myself up for dumping my kit.

My gaze was focused constantly on the horizon, scanning for any sign of the South Pole station. I knew that to reach it, I'd have to cycle around the airfield, diverting my journey south, off to the right a little. With less than 40 kilometres to go, it was still not in my line of sight, and I wondered if I would make it by tonight. I felt tired, and having taken the maximum recommended painkillers, I was also running out of options for pain control. I put my iPod back on.

It felt like an eternity, and then suddenly, I spotted a flash of light that looked like the reflection of sun rays. I gazed with all my might, straining my eyes, but I still couldn't see anything but total whiteness. Another hour passed before I could focus on a black dot on the horizon. It was the South Pole Station. I had just 19 kilometres to go.

The moment I saw the South Pole Station for the first time, my body began a shutdown process, and everything became even more challenging. My tired muscles were weakening, and my knee pain was even worse. I cried with sadness, pain and despair. I was so close, yet so far. I still had another three or four hours of cycling to go, as my speed was dropping dramatically. Would I make it?

It wasn't only me who had invested much precious time and effort into this expedition; Wayne, Emil, and Torfi had all given up their time to support me. It was now a record for all of us. Even though I would be the first to cycle to the South Pole, it was by no means a mission I had completed alone. It was a massive team effort. I even felt the support of my parents sitting back home, willing me to succeed, as they watched my tracking device resonate from many thousands of miles away. I could feel everyone's support and couldn't let them down now.

I comforted myself with the fact that my formula had been right to get this far. The path chosen was right, and all obstacles that had appeared in the way, not just during the last ten days but from the previous four years, had been mastered.

The very concept of near achievement fascinated me. I could see my goal ahead, gradually metamorphosing from a spec in the snow into a more defined shape, yet I still couldn't fight off the occasional flash through my mind of what if I don't make it. As I pedalled closer, blinking and staring at the looming outline, every five minutes felt like an hour, and every kilometre took longer to cycle. I was pushing through treacle that was turning to cement.

"I'm really struggling," I said to Emil at one of my rest stops. "I can't feel my feet, and I'm delirious with pain. I'm not sure how much my body can take," I continued in a shaky voice.

"You're nearly there," Emil said quietly. "Focus on the station."

Emil had a calming influence on me. He rarely gave an opinion, though I sensed he, too, was hugely relieved that the end goal was in sight. After two months in Antarctica, he was as keen as me to get home.

"I need to increase the frequency of my rest stops," I told Emil.

I was down to stopping every three kilometres. Then Emil would drive up alongside me to watch as I slowly and painfully levered myself from the seat of the Polar Cycle to the ground to try and warm up my feet and gain a little more strength to continue. Earlier in the expedition, I would pee at every rest stop, yet during this 17-hour day of cycling, I had only peed once. My bodily functions were beginning to shut down. I knew the feeling all too well from long adventure races. I was nearing my limit. The fact that the end was so near accelerated the shutting-down process.

My stops were three minutes long. I had no appetite, and my stomach would revolt at every piece of food I put in my mouth. I was shivering uncontrollably, internally and externally. My vision was blurring, partly due to the build-up of mist in my goggles but also due to sleep deprivation and extreme physical exertion. I had to really focus on not passing out. I bowed my head and stared at my right knee. I tried to use the power of my mind to remove the pain that was exploding from my kneecap. I attempted to visualise the pain being dispelled into the air. As the pain floated away, I, too, floated with it.

I took myself to my safe place on a magical lake in the Swedish archipelago, which I use when times are tough. I float on a small wooden boat with a white sail. The boat is filled with an array of different coloured cushions, and I lie gazing up at the clear blue sky with the occasional bird gliding way up above. I look at the heather-covered slopes interspersed with tall pine trees surrounding the lake. There are blueberries in the woodland. I wish I could pick the shiny black fruit concealed in the voluminous bushes. For a few seconds, I'm in heaven.

Then reality reverberates like a punch in the stomach, but it's enough for me to cover another kilometre. I can just make out the full outline of the South Pole station now. There is activity. I can see vehicles moving around. It looks like they are shifting crates. I'm almost there.

With just six kilometres to go, I was in for a surprise. The South Pole station received two flights a week, and one was due to arrive any minute. It was 2 am UK time. Emil crept up alongside me in his truck. "I've just called the station, and we need to wait for an hour and a half for the plane to land, drop off passengers and then take off again," he said. My timing couldn't have been more inconvenient, and the thought of stopping filled me with fear. Would my body completely shut down, and would I be able to get going again?

During the expedition, I had not allowed myself to look back because my motivation had to be forward and positive, never allowing for an inch of doubt. For only the second time in the expedition, I turned around to look behind me. My eyes met a blazing whiteness with no differentiation between the sky and snow. It was a cloudy day, and everything merged into one. I stepped off the Polar Cycle in agony and hobbled around it. I struggled to stand up and lurched uncontrollably, trying to gain my balance. It felt like my body had frozen in a seated position, and I couldn't control my limbs. I forced myself to repeatedly walk around the Polar Cycle until I had oiled the muscles sufficiently to sense a slow but painful release. Looking ahead, I could see the end was in sight, but strangely, I was being pulled away from it like the rebound of a bungee run. Six kilometres stood between me and the title, and I was in a situation I could not control. It was a forced stop, and I hated being told what to do. Did no one understand the magnitude of my mission and my urgency to complete it?

I considered diverting my path to veer around the South Pole station, but Emil was quick to pull me up on the fact that when the South Pole Station issue an order not to enter the perimeter of the station, then it is not taken too kindly if one is found trespassing. A quick mathematical calculation in my head also worked out that going around the runway and heading into the South Pole from a 180-degree position from where I was would add a further 19 kilometres—far too much to cope with in my condition. Instead, I served my waiting sentence, anxiously watching the seconds tick by on my wristwatch.

There was not a single metre I hadn't pedalled so far, and now I had only a few kilometres left. If I continued like this, I could claim I was the first person to cycle to the South Pole. I would feel true to myself that I really had achieved this record. All I needed to do now was complete this mammoth task.

After a frustrating one-and-a-half-hour wait, it was time for my final six kilometres to the South Pole. Both trucks shot off to the South Pole so they could film my arrival. The going was extremely uncomfortable as I negotiated caterpillar tracks created by the vehicles operating out of the South Pole. As I pushed the very last ounce of energy out of my

154

exhausted body, I began to sweat profusely, but for the first time in the expedition, I didn't deal with it. Every other time, I had religiously removed some layers of clothes or slowed down to allow my body to regulate itself, as I knew sweating in polar climates was a potential killer. With less than an hour of pedalling ahead of me, I was letting go, and I no longer thought like a polar adventurer.

During the last couple of kilometres, I passed a stockpile of crates used to transport goods to the South Pole. In my dream-like state, they appeared like an omen that I was being transported back to life on Earth. The silence was broken when a skidoo, pulling a trailer, suddenly drove up alongside me with a band of scientists on board shouting and waving. Instinctively, but on reflection rather ridiculously, I looked around to see if they were waving to someone behind me. There was, of course, no one else around and certainly no one else who had cycled from the continent's edge to the South Pole.

The skidoo carried five American scientists who had been watching my approach on their computer screens from the warmth of their South Pole office. They were now coming to congratulate me and cheer me on my very last lap! They clapped their hands, and their raised voices sounded noisy and unreal, interrupting my silent world.

I was cycling in a dream on remote control, and suddenly and strangely, the end seemed to rush towards me at an amazing pace. I will never forget the surge of excitement that filled my exhausted body as I grasped the ice-cold South Pole globe marker in my arms, hugging it momentarily and letting out a scream.

It was early morning on December 27, and it had taken me 10 days, 14 hours, and 56 minutes to become the first person to cycle to the South Pole. I had pedalled every metre of the way.

# 18. Two World Records

## "When incredible things seem normal, it's time to reassess"

Y ou've just cycled into the history books," Wayne shouted as he filmed my arrival at the South Pole marker. Reaching my goal released an uncontrollable surge of happiness in me. I will never forget that moment. I had reached my goal and earned a world record.

My four years of preparation culminated in one moment. At the same time, it felt odd. Something that I had been so committed to and focused on for four years was now over. I felt lost and unsure of what to do next. Was it really me who had arrived at my destination, or was I in the middle of one of those nagging nightmares that had plagued my preparations? In my exhausted, confused state, it was hard to distinguish reality. My mind flashed back to when I approached the Leverett Glacier and the fear encompassing my body. It felt like a lifetime ago. Had I climbed it yet? Now, the only memory of the whole journey was my excruciating knee pain.

I was unable to release my grasp of the South Pole marker. My reflexes would not reason with me, even though I felt the cold of the metal seeping through my three layers of gloves. I had to hold on to ensure that I had arrived. I needed time for my mind to understand that I had made it.

Wayne came over to me and lifted me into his arms. To begin with, I could not support my body weight, and my knee seemed frozen into an oddly bent shape. The pain was worse than ever. "You've done it, well done, you're incredible," Wayne whispered. I tried to respond, but my lips were dry and stuck together. I didn't know what to say. I had just achieved a life-long ambition, yet I was worrying about our relationship. I held onto him. We both had excited emotions for many reasons, but were they for the most important ones?

I could sense his relief that the expedition was over. At last, a homebound trip for us both. He was relieved that I was safe and that he would no longer need to sit in a truck for hours every day as I pounded the pedals against my body's wishes.

Strangely, I was so uncontrollably excited about what I had achieved that my emotions felt paralysed. The end was so confusing. "What now?" I thought as we embraced each other in the middle of Antarctica. I don't believe either of us knew the answer.

The Amundsen-Scott South Pole Station, situated at the South Pole, appeared incongruous with neatly arranged metal containers lined on the snow, all looking like they shouldn't be there. Its modern aerodynamic design was like an inharmonious growth in the whiteness. The main building was elevated above the surface of the Antarctic ice sheet that lay up to four kilometres thick. Its unique construction, designed to be hydraulically raised to extend the station's useful life, allowed blowing snow to pass underneath it.

How different and empty it must have seemed to Roald Amundsen and his four fellow Norwegians, who arrived here in mid-December 1911 to raise the Norwegian flag and claim a world first. And how disheartening it must have been for Captain Scott, arriving a month later with British Terra Nova expedition members. I reflected on Scott's words upon reaching the Pole: "Great God! This is an awful place" which likely stood in stark contrast to Amundsen's stoic sense of satisfaction and achievement. Both sentiments were so true, reflecting Antarctica's vicious yet beautiful nature—a place I had come to see from both perspectives.

For today's scientists and support staff, during the long Antarctic winter, a period characterised by extreme cold, perpetual darkness, and fierce storms. During this time, weather conditions deteriorate so severely that no aircraft can land, effectively isolating the station's inhabitants from the rest of the world.

The ceremonial South Pole marker was surrounded by the flags of the original 12 signatory nations to the Antarctic Treaty and lay just outside the South Pole station. With my very last ounce of energy, I hobbled, with Wayne taking most of my weight, to the warmth of the South Pole station, where I was thrilled to receive the South Pole station stamp on my passport. I was even invited to place the stamp in my passport myself. It was a mark of my success, my recognition of arrival and my medal of achievement.

The South Pole station felt strange—a sudden imposter to the silent, empty world to which I had become accustomed. The high altitude didn't affect me in the same way as it had earlier. My lung capacity had adapted to the squeeze on oxygen, but the suppressive feel was clearly present in the atmosphere.

The expedition company, ALE, had a camp a few kilometres from the South Pole where Wayne, Emil, Torfi, and I settled in to allow ourselves a chance to rest and eat. We put up our tent solemnly, as did Emil and Torfi. We were all shattered and spoke very little.

Without realising it, I had achieved not one but two world records: one for being the first person in history to cycle from the edge of the Antarctic continent to the South Pole and the second for setting the most incredible human-powered speed record of 10 days, 14 hours, and 56 minutes.

For many years, the Norwegian Christian Eide held the fastest human-powered journey in 24 days, 1 hour and 13 minutes. Then, two days before my record, a young American, led by Doug Stoup, set the human-powered record at 18 days. I had now taken that down to just under 11 days. A double world record—I could hardly believe it!

We had 48 hours remaining at the South Pole before returning northward. Our journey back would involve travelling by truck via the frequently used route to Hercules Inlet, leading to Union Glacier. This trip was expected to last an additional three days. Although tired and aching, I felt totally in my element, loving the experience while Wayne was possibly in his worst place. I wanted the experience to last longer, but Wayne was more than ready to go home. With such different perspectives on life, I prayed we could see this one through.

I reminisced that the Polar Cycle had not let me down. Every nut, bolt and screw had remained firmly in place, and my chain had survived the worst. My tyres, despite accounting for much of the weight, did manage to give me the float needed when the going was tough, and my decision to use ice studs on the Leverett Glacier had been the right choice. I was also pleased that on the fourth night, I sacrificed many hours of sleep to remove the ice studs because, on the Polar Plateau, the snow was sticking to them and badly impeding my progress.

It was now 3 am GMT, but it was late afternoon at the South Pole station, which was working in NZ time. There were three other tents at the camp housing expeditioners and a slightly larger logistics tent, where we were warmly welcomed for a meal the next morning. The ALE camp was operating in yet another time zone—Chilean time so we ate an evening meal for breakfast. It tasted wonderful all the same. I was delighted to sit next to Doug Stoup, a world-leading polar pioneer and guide who had just led a ski expedition to the South Pole. Funnily enough, I was wearing my polar boots, aptly named Doug Stoup.

"You're a legend. Can we have a photo together at the South Pole," he said. I couldn't believe that this incredible polar pioneer was referring to me.

Given my massive spurt over the last few days of the expedition, the pressure was relieved, and we were now in good time for the trucks to be back at base to prepare for over-wintering. We decided to go to Union Glacier by truck to catch our departing flight from Antarctica instead of flying. The three-day truck journey along the Hercules Inlet route to Union Glacier, allowing for rest time, meant we would arrive just in time for New Year's Eve. After spending Christmas Day on the Polar Cycle, I was relieved, more so for Wayne, Torfi and Emil, that they would not have to sit in a truck and silently do a 3-2-1 'Happy New Year' countdown to themselves.

It felt odd to be inside a warm, moving truck, and I soon began to long for the biting cold that I had learnt to live with for so long. I now had to go through a whole new programme of acclimatisation in reverse. Heated to 18 degrees Celsius, the truck felt claustrophobic, and my cheeks were burning up. Still, I enjoyed the conversation with Emil as the trucks bounced solidly from side to side, negotiating the uneven ice surface. My knee felt like a balloon, so I packed ice around my kneecap each time we stopped briefly.

Emil had driven across Antarctica before, but it was his first time to take the Leverett Glacier route. He talked about the Walking with the Wounded expedition that he had transported and how hard it had been for the soldiers. Three teams of wounded servicemen and women from the UK, the US, Australia and Canada walked from 3° to the geographic South Pole. Weather conditions were so fierce that, at one point, the teams had to be driven forward several hundred metres before they could resume their trek. "The bravery of those soldiers was amazing, and I was so impressed with how Prince Harry related to and supported each of them," said Emil.

He was also slightly amused when Prince Harry regularly went up to his driver's window to ask to use his satellite phone so he could call his girlfriend back home.

Emil had a good word for me, too, which boosted my morale no end. "You are a great role model for my daughters, especially in the way you push on despite the odds against you," he said. I felt elated.

After a day and a half of travel, we came across the first of the other two cyclists who had been aiming to claim the title. We stopped the truck, and the Spaniard, Juan Menendez Granados, shook my hand and chatted to me with much grace. "Well done," he said weakly. He looked exhausted and withdrawn, and Emil immediately offered to top up his freeze-dried rations from his stores. "No, I'm ok," he said. "I'm hoping to complete this unsupported. The route has been really tough, so I have had to do a lot of skiing," he said.

It must have been earth-shattering for him to learn of my success, yet surprisingly, he remained composed. Juan completed his 46-day expedition reaching the South Pole using skis and a fat bike on January 17, 2014.

Half a day later, while I snoozed in the truck, Emil spotted the American dragging his bike. He was clearly having a difficult cycle ride. Daniel Burton of Eagle Mountain arrived at the geographic South Pole on January 21, 2014, on a fat bike after cycling some of the journey.

We stopped to take photos of the isolated Theil Mountain Range as we skirted it in the truck before we headed down to Union Glacier. We saw a dark blob on the horizon that disturbed the pristine whiteness of the surroundings. It was a food drop for some expedition groups skiing to the Pole. Even though my expedition was over, Wayne and I spoke very little. Words felt meaningless and empty, and I was in a strange, transient world. We sat in separate vehicles, and I constantly worried about how we would pick our relationship up again. Was this the end?

We arrived at Union Glacier, the logistics hub for Antarctica, in the early afternoon, where Fran, part of the ALE logistics team, warmly welcomed us. It was a huge camp with many double-walled sleeping tents with large doors and high interiors, which was different from my cramped one-person tent. They also had a wooden floor underneath to provide insulation from the snow. The larger dining tents were appropriately named after the ships Terra Nova and Fram, which Scott and Amundsen had sailed into Antarctica. There were rows of smaller tents where scientists lived during the season.

Here, we spent New Year's Eve with scientists and ALE logistics staff in an ice cave that the staff had dug out for the past few days. I felt privileged to be in an ice cave in one of the most majestical places on Earth. Vicious though it was, I greatly respected Antarctica's beauty and purity.

After consuming a small can of lager, which had cost ALE approximately £8 to buy it, fly it in, then fly the empty can back out again, some one-legged hopping in an ice cave and some more friends to add to my address book, it was time for bed. Wayne and I were still passing frosty comments back and forth. While I was revelling in life in such extremes, he was desperate to leave. How could we be thinking so differently? My idea of a perfect holiday was to be in snowy mountains skiing or biking, and Wayne's dream was to be in tropical climates boating, fishing or relaxing in the sun. How could we make this work?

The following day was my first opportunity for a medical check. My general condition was good, and I'd lost just over 8% of my body weight. The medic told me that most people came back from expeditions as skin and bone, so I was delighted with my body's endurance. It had been in rapid decline towards the end, but, for the best part, it stood up well to the challenge.

My knee was a different story. It desperately needed rest. Due to repetitive strain injury and a lack of synovial fluid, which was essential for frictionless movement, my kneecap had been grinding away like a rusty pepper grinder. If left untreated, the medic warned, it could ultimately impair my knee's movement, and in severe cases, the fluid loss could cause osteoarthritis.

I drowned my concern by having my first shower for three weeks. It was housed in a tin hut with six cubicles and solar panels on the roof that heated the water. I took a bucket of water with holes in the bottom and hung it on a hook. It was one of the best forty seconds of my life.

As I stood partially refreshed after the brief shower, I couldn't stop thinking, what next? I was not in a physical state to take on anything new yet, but to control my adventure-seeking mind, I had to begin to make plans. Seeing a few skiers and climbers leaving Union Glacier and heading out on their own expeditions made me yearn for more, and I set myself on a mission to head north next time, either by bike or skis.

Goal setting has always satisfied me, mainly because it empowered me with a task I had to see through to the end. Whether it was trying to overtake the person in front of me during my morning run or scaling a mountainside, there was a definite beginning and end but no clear route. Giving up halfway was not an option. On the occasions when I was forced to give up in races, I was deflated and disappointed, but it somehow fuelled my determination to do better next time. That annoying word 'can't' refuses to resonate in my vocabulary. Whatever obstacles block my path, there is still a way forward. There are so many sides to a story and many paths to follow, and I am determined to seek them out. If one doesn't work, there is a good chance that another will work and turn out to be the best option. What happens happens for a good reason.

Perhaps this drive lies in my problem-solving nature, which was nurtured by my maths teacher all those years ago. He brought a sparkle to my day with his comical teaching techniques and demonstrated that with persistence, you can find the answer. It's also about having confidence in yourself; if you are fully prepared, you are halfway there.

As Wayne left the shower cubicle, newly shaven, I saw a small spark return in him. I could sense his relief that we were on our way home.

I realised it had been as tough for him as it was for me but in a different way. Seeing me struggle in pain, the risks I took cycling up the glacier, sitting for endless hours and days in a bumpy truck, with the knowledge that every time he stepped outside, the biting wind would chill him to the core—and unlike me, he hated the cold. It had been a massive ask, but we had come through the dark moments, and we had a world record to look back on.

On January 4th, we took off from the frozen runway at Union Glacier inbound to Punta Arenas in Chile. My almost complete circumnavigation of the globe via the South Pole had nearly come to an end, and as I gazed out over the vast icy plains of Antarctica, I vowed to myself that I would return one day.

Three months later, I found myself sitting on the start line of the Devizes to Westminster International Canoe Race in a K2 boat with my friend Nicola. Fortunately, sitting in the boat meant it wasn't a challenge for my knee, which was healing very slowly. The 125-mile race over 27 non-stop hours was, as expected, painful, emotional, beautiful and all for the medal around our necks at the end.

My relationship with Wayne had gone from strength to strength. The frosty relationship we had shared sometimes during our time in Antarctica had well and truly thawed. During a romantic trip to Venice, I was presented with the most beautiful diamond engagement ring, which sparkled brightly and had a blue shimmer. It was only a matter of weeks before we could share the news with family that I was pregnant. The next chapter of my life had begun.

On this journey, I was a beginner. What if I didn't know how to be a mother? What if I couldn't manage the birth? What if my baby didn't like me? For nine months, I suppressed my concerns in my 'Day by Day Guide to Pregnancy' book, which I used as my bible, reading it over and over again.

Strangely, I was experiencing emotions similar to those I had in the lead-up to and during my South Pole expedition. It needed planning and preparation, but, more importantly, positive, powerful 'can-do thinking.'

Over the years, I have learnt that there are three types of reactions to pain. The first is acting too late in response to pain, which I can say happily I have not reached (nor do I ever want to). Ultimately, it means pushing yourself so hard that your body and mind reach their limit, and in worse-case scenarios, it ends in death. The second type is where you push very hard and achieve incredible things by nearing your limit, and the third is when you succumb too soon and regret not achieving what you believe you could achieve.

Knowing where to draw the line is the challenge. I realised my body was a brilliant machine and always listened to it. I had been through some harrowing times, but I had managed to differentiate between when my body was close to shutting down and when my mind had exaggerated that pain. The common denominator was my level of fear. If I was fearful, then I hurt more. Only experience had helped me to manage my fear of pain.

I enrolled myself on some hypnobirthing sessions, which helped me live in the moment and reinforced the message that I must not fear pain. I knew I was strong and wanted to show my baby I was strong, too. I used colour therapy techniques, where I practised visualising the colour yellow wrapped around me and my baby, which helped me feel warm and secure. Wayne bought me a beautiful yellow scarf, one of the colours of the Swedish flag, and I held it in front of my eyes during my meditation sessions to help bring the visualisation to life. I was facing another endurance challenge and felt convinced I would succeed.

'It's a girl!' Wayne said. Klara was lifted and placed on my chest. "I'm your mummy," I whispered, tears streaming down my face. I was overwhelmed with pride. The moments of pain when I could have easily lost control were managed by my powerful mantra, "I can do this. It's perfectly normal to feel this way."

I recalled my joy in reaching the South Pole and achieving a world record. Becoming a mother was very different, but just as emotional.

Always in the back of my mind are plans for my next expedition. Klara regularly comes out with me in the pram while I run, on the bike seat between my arms as I cycle, or in the sling while I hike. And that yellow scarf hangs next to Klara's cot, hoping it will give her the strength to believe she can achieve anything she dreams.

The invisible circle principle, pivotal during my polar expedition, now guides me daily. When faced with daunting or complex challenges, I simplify them by focusing only on what's within my control. I share this empowering strategy in school talks, encouraging students and my daughters alike to use it as a compass through life's complexities.

The situation, our interactions, and the unpredictability of technological progress shape our emotions. These can amplify stress, but recognising what we can influence provides a clear direction. By differentiating the controllable from the uncontrollable, we avoid the trap of inevitable failure and channel our energy into actions that steer us toward our goals.

# 19. Ten Years On - A Return to the South Pole

"The only impossible journey is the one you never begin"
— Tony Robbins.

E arlier in my story, I referred to this witty paradox attributed to Oscar Wilde: "Everything in moderation, including moderation." So, it seemed fitting that, in the early hours of December 17, 2023, I found myself at Pembroke Dock in a queue of cars and lorries under a drizzly, dark sky, about to board a ferry aptly named 'Oscar Wilde'.

This time, I was not setting out alone. My good friend Nick enthusiastically agreed to accompany me when I mentioned my plan earlier in the year. Nick shares a love of cold, remote places and has also spent time in the Arctic and Antarctic. He's a geologist, photographer and co-founder of the website Snow-Forecast.com. By sheer coincidence, his company donated to my Alzheimer's charity fundraiser in 2013 when I was searching so hard for sponsors to fund my cycle to the South Pole.

Amidst the rumble of engines, our presence was an anomaly, for we were the only ones on mountain bikes. The Oscar Wilde was bound for Rosslare, in south-east Ireland. I intended to mark ten years of reaching the actual South Pole by cycling over 300 kilometres to the South Pole Inn in the tiny village of Annascaul on the Dingle Peninsula, County Kerry.

The South Pole Inn has become a pilgrimage site for those fascinated by the history of polar exploration. It was established in

1920 by the Antarctic explorer Tom Crean. Crean's experiences in Antarctica are a powerful testament to human endurance and the quest for exploration, characterised by his participation in three significant expeditions spanning over a decade.

He joined the crew of Scott's Discovery Expedition (1901-1904) and returned to Antarctica once more for Scott's tragic Terra Nova Expedition (1910-1913), performing a dangerous solo trek to save the life of Lieutenant Edward Evans. His most legendary endeavours unfolded as part of Sir Ernest Shackleton's Imperial Trans-Antarctic Expedition (1914-1917), a venture to achieve Antarctica's first land crossing. After Shackleton's ship, the Endurance, was trapped and eventually crushed by the relentless pack ice of the Weddell Sea, the expedition's crew was left stranded on the shore of Elephant Island. Shackleton devised a daring rescue plan to secure the survival of all 28 stranded men.

Crean, Shackleton and four others embarked on a perilous 800-mile journey across the Southern Ocean in the small, ill-equipped lifeboat James Caird. Battling monstrous seas, freezing temperatures, and the constant threat of capsizing, their triumphant arrival on the rugged shores of South Georgia is cited as one of the most incredible small boat journeys ever undertaken.

After landing on the wrong side of South Georgia, the men endured an arduous overland journey without maps, using a carpenter's adze, rope, and sheer determination to navigate uncharted terrain. They eventually reached the whaling station at Stromness to arrange the rescue of the remaining expedition members, who had survived for over four months under an upturned boat on Elephant Island.

Celebrated for his remarkable survival capabilities, robust strength, and guiding presence, Crean's heroic deeds and knack for uplifting spirits in dire situations have secured his status as one of Ireland's most extraordinary, unsung heroes.

Crean returned to Ireland in 1920, embracing a quieter life far removed from the ice and snow that had defined his earlier years. When Sir Ernest Shackleton was organising another Antarctic expedition, Crean respectfully declined the invitation to join, remarking that he now had a "long-haired pal"—an affectionate reference to his new wife, Ellen Herlihy. His marriage marked the beginning of a new chapter as landlord of the South Pole Inn.

Here, Crean's reputation for warmth and hospitality grew. The pub was a gathering place for locals and travellers alike; Crean remained modest, preferring to listen to others rather than recount his past glories. The walls of the pub, both in the past and still today, resonate with the tales of his adventures and those of many other heroic polar explorers.

I originally intended to begin my ride to the South Pole Inn from a point closer to home, the tiny coastal Welsh village of Rhossili on the Gower Peninsula. This is where Petty Officer Edgar Evans was born in 1876 and died at age 35, almost 10,000 miles away at the foot of the Beardmore Glacier in Antarctica on the return from the South Pole with Captain Scott.

There was little time to plan, pack or train for my 10th-anniversary challenge, so the Welsh start would have to wait for another day. Still, between being a full-time mother to my two young daughters, running two businesses, and hurried Christmas shopping, I'd managed to read the excellent biography "An Unsung Hero: Tom Crean - Antarctic Survivor," having previously met the author Michael Smith after a talk he delivered to the Captain Scott Society in Cardiff.

Carrying the knowledge of this quiet giant of a man encouraged me to believe that our journey across his native Ireland to meet him in spirit, whilst insignificant in comparison, proved anything was possible. As I'd found time and time again, mental strength makes up many times over for lack of physical preparedness.

Nick and I quietly disembarked from the ferry into the blustery darkness of Rosslare ferry terminal and were shocked to be greeted not once but twice by the visage of Tom Crean. The encounter wasn't a hallucination from lack of sleep but the result of local cyclists Brian and Michael from Wexford joining us for the start of our ride after hearing of our arrival. Their cycling club jerseys paid homage to Tom Crean, featuring his face on the back.

Compared to the Scott Scale hardtail mountain bikes we were riding, laden with food, sleeping mats and spares, Brian and Michael's road bikes set a mean pace, faster than I'd planned for the early stage of the ride. As we left the streetlights of Rosslare behind, we turned west into a strengthening headwind, and their cheerful chat provided a welcome distraction. Just as I felt a rhythm to the ride set in, Brian insisted we stop for a photo opportunity at the gates of Chris de Burgh's castle. He seemed so proud of this landmark that it seemed rude not to indulge, so we dismounted, posed under a large sign saying 'private', and resumed our ride as the first light turned the hedgerows into dark silhouettes.

One of my adventure racing contacts supplied a GPS tracker that enabled our real-time progress to be followed online as a tiny dot on the map of Ireland. Brian said he'd keep an eye out and assured us that his friend Jimmy, CFO of Hertz Ireland, would be available if anything went terribly wrong. So, with the tune of "Lady in Red" incessantly playing in my head, we said goodbye to our new friends and left them looking for a coffee shop in Bridgetown.

Finally, we were alone, and I could contemplate this exact time ten years ago when I departed from the Ross Ice Shelf toward the South Pole on the Polar Cycle, my mind awash with a similar exhilaration and focus that had propelled me to my goal. Given the hectic nature of life with all its uncertainties, it seemed remarkable that I could relive my adventure again on a bike and fulfil my ambition of going to the South Pole Inn.

On the ferry, I'd scribbled down a rough plan for places to stop and refuel to reach the South Pole Inn at 11 am the following morning. It went like this:

Start at Rosslare ferry terminal on December 17, 2023, at 7 am, and catch the 9 am ferry at Ballyhack. Continue to Waterford after about 70 km and take a break in Cappoquin at the 125 km point. Proceed to Mallow, reaching it after 187 km, then plan to rest overnight in a woodland near Newmarket at the 215 km mark. The following day, continue our journey, passing through Castleisland at 250 km and Castlemaine at 270 km, before completing the 320 km cycle at the South Pole Inn at 11 am on December 18.

We reached the Ballyhack car ferry on time. This short crossing of the River Barrow would take us from County Wexford into County Waterford and save some miles by avoiding the need to head inland.

We were well dressed for the weather conditions, but with the temperature hovering around 9 degrees Celsius, the wind chill caused us to cool down and shiver within a few minutes each time we stopped. Behind a heavy glass door, the ferry had a small, heated cabin for foot passengers that smelled of gloss paint. This provided a moment of comfort before it was time to get back on the bikes and climb the first steep hill of the ride.

The green country lanes gave way to the main roads and roundabouts of the Waterford suburbs. A small shopping centre seemed an excellent place to stop for a hearty breakfast. Just as we were putting on our damp outer layers, a timely message from Brian suggested that, considering the deteriorating weather, we would be better off taking the Waterford Greenway rather than our planned coastal route.

The Greenway is a cycle and walking trail stretching over 50 kilometres along an old railway track that once connected Waterford City with the coastal town of Dungarvan. It was nice to be away from traffic, but the brutal 35 km/h headwinds drastically slowed our pace. We took turns riding in front and breaking the wind, and I was pleased each time Nick suggested we stop and indulge in a little variety in the form of a giant box of Haribo jelly bears purchased from the duty-free shop on the ferry.

Cycling across Antarctica and cycling to the South Pole Inn both shared a single purpose of getting from A to B by the most efficient means. As such, there was little opportunity for interesting detours, luxury, or anything else, which was good.

The route through Ireland mainly consisted of muddy fields, tiny hamlets, and isolated villas, many of which seemed disproportionately grand compared to their surroundings. Making the journey at Christmas meant that welcome interest was added by festive lights and decorations in many of the homes and towns, with Fermoy and Lismore being the most memorable.

The joy of being on a bike with the sole purpose of simply heading toward a distant goal is unique and precious. It provides an escape from the complexities of daily life and, with those removed, allows one to enjoy a simple sense of being in the moment. At these times, connectedness with nature heightens, and the wind, rain, wildlife and scenery all seem closer and more vivid.

My plan had allowed longer stops to eat and rest, but many places were closed (it was a Sunday), and our eagerness to make the most of our good progress meant we paused for no more than half an hour at a time to eat the snacks we were carrying. This worked well until we approached the market town of Mallow.

Darkness had set in about an hour before, and I noticed Nick looking pale and tired a few hundred meters back, constantly changing his position and grip on the bike. We took a break at a converted horse box serving as a trendy coffee shop, trying to rest by a loud generator on a muddy verge whilst consuming coffee and snacks. The periods of silence between us had grown longer, and it was becoming apparent that we needed to reconsider our rest and refuel strategy.

By the time we crossed a festively lit bridge over the Blackwater River and entered the heart of Mallow, we'd accumulated 187 kilometres since starting earlier that same day. Apart from a restaurant that looked way too classy for people in our condition, we reluctantly walked into a petrol station with little to offer besides the ubiquitous chocolate bars, crisps and insipid sandwiches. I asked the man on the counter if they had anything else, and he presented a tray of croissants, saying they'd been out all day and we could take what we wanted for free. I took four, then glancing up, spotted a brightly lit American diner over the road.

Before entering, we stowed the bikes in an alley behind some smelly industrial food bins. The clatter of our sodden cycling shoes on the greasy floor caused a few of the families dining there to pause mid-mouthful and contemplate these two mumbling, zombie-like figures who placed a random food order before collapsing onto a bright red cushioned bench seat by the steamy window. All we could think of was rest, but I knew from bitter experience that getting comfortable at this point of a journey could spell the premature end of it. More than a couple hours' sleep means the body goes into repair mode, making it much harder to keep going when we wake up.

Nick admitted afterwards that he had a secret bail-out plan in case things went wrong and we risked missing our deadline at the South Pole Inn. Mallow had a station, and a 7:30 pm train to Tralee would save us 90 kilometres or five more hours of cycling.

After some food and drink, our conversation became more coherent, and we agreed the only option was to keep going but find somewhere to rest after eating. This experience corroborates research, which definitively states that having a backup plan often affects the chances of success for the initial plan.

After an hour in Mallow, we pressed on into what was now a cold, starlit night, looking for a shelter to get some sleep. County Cork lacked the more frequent derelict houses and farm buildings we saw so many of at the start of our ride. I hadn't long returned from an 800-kilometre race across the Eastern Cape of South Africa, where I'd spent a memorable night in sub-zero temperatures on the floor of an abattoir wearing little more than a foil blanket, so my bar for quality accommodation was set pretty low!

It was raining again, so Nick's suggestion of a bunker on the 18th hole of Mallow Golf Course seemed less practical. After a steep descent into darkness, the way ahead was cheerfully illuminated by a Christmas tree outside a pub called Fitzgerald's. We dismounted, and I rattled the doors of some outbuildings, all locked. Nick had the bright idea of going in and asking if the pub would let us lie down under a shelter in the beer garden. So, trying to assume the pose of people just going out for an evening drink, we shuffled up to the bar.

The man behind the bar was a large, red-faced man with an impressive moustache. I explained that we were cycling to the South

Pole Inn from Rosslare and wondered if we could lie down somewhere for a couple of hours. I'll never forget his response. The other guests fell silent, then mid-pulling a pint of Guinness, he paused and stared intently at the two of us. Then, as if we didn't exist, he continued what he was doing, and the background noise resumed. I had half a mind that he would turn on us and shout, "Get out of my fecking pub now…" but instead, he disappeared into a back room.

Shortly, a welcoming woman approached us, radiating kindness, and insisted that we couldn't sleep outside. She offered us the back lounge, which was not in use, to make ourselves at home. When I mentioned we needed to be back on the road by 1 am, she reassured us it was not a problem as that was their closing time.

Two hours later, she reappeared with two cups of instant coffee and the offer of toast. Sensing our deadline in ten hours, we politely declined and, after grateful farewells, continued on our way. At that point, Nick exclaimed we were 3 kilometres EAST of Mallow! We'd been so tired that after our stop in the American diner, we'd headed out in totally the opposite direction. That turned out to be a kind twist of fate, as the road from Mallow to Newmarket was remarkable in being unremarkable, with no possible place for rest.

Newmarket, 215 kilometres into the trip, was the next stop on our plan. We'd run out of water at this point, and a distant lack of Christmas decorations seemed to add to the general sense that at 3 am, we were the only people not cosily in bed. Completely failing in the search for a tap, we settled on some steps in the lee of the front wall of Little Treasures Pre-School to tuck into the croissants we'd been gifted the previous evening.

At this point in the journey, it became noticeable to us both that our stops, though still short, were becoming more frequent, and the sustenance of jelly bears and chocolate bars was proving increasingly short-lived.

Ballydesmond was so small we didn't actually notice it, although it did mark the onset of the biggest hills in the remotest part of our corner of Ireland. These weren't particularly difficult; using different muscles to climb was nice. But tiredness was becoming unavoidable, and I started to nod off behind the handlebars. I thought about how cosy I was ten years ago in my little red tent in Antarctica and how my rituals carried out were a welcome change to the monotony. Seeing a sign ahead reading Jones Agri Ltd., I had no choice but to pull over.

I wandered semi-deliriously around their yard looking for water, perplexed by the numerous dispensers that were demonstration cattle water troughs not connected to the mains. Nick appeared and pointed out the unlocked toilet right before me, which I refilled before falling asleep, resting on a dusty concrete floor, my head in his lap. After what felt a lot more than ten minutes, he urged us to get back on the bikes.

The road resembled a roller coaster of steep climbs and descents, and this time, it was Nick who abruptly halted the lead, saying he was now falling asleep and didn't feel safe. We stopped at a junction opposite a lonely grey and white house and spotted a concrete barn with a red corrugated iron roof. For once, it wasn't locked, and the wooden door slid to one side, revealing a dry but cluttered interior.

I found a rolled-up carpet and dust sheet that brought a touch of relative luxury to the situation. The timing couldn't have been better as we lay down, torrential rain hammered on the tin roof, and we fell asleep instantly. Although it was around 6 degrees Celsius, the warmth of our bodies proved more than enough, and when my alarm went off an hour later, we both felt genuinely refreshed and ready for the final leg to the South Pole Inn.

The rain eased as we started the next climb but returned with a vengeance as we quickly descended into Castleisland. We didn't pause long enough to appreciate the town's widest street in Ireland, longest cave system or fame for producing talented basketball players. We pressed on for the penultimate leg in Castlemaine.

Castlemaine is known as the Gateway to the Dingle Peninsula, but the only gateway we were interested in at 8 am was the door to the warmly lit local store. It was one of those shops that seemed to sell everything one could need for any situation, but all we could think of was coffee and breakfast rolls. The owner looked at us inquisitively as I explained that we'd cycled across Ireland from Rosslare the morning before. He listened patiently before grabbing a large bag of rubbish and walking past us, shaking his head and muttering.

We had been looking forward to what promised to be a beautiful final leg along the coastal road of the south Dingle Peninsula, but once again, the weather had the upper hand. Dense fog meant the only hint of being by the sea was the sound of the crashing surf at Inch Strand and salty spray in our faces. The straight road went on and on, and the time of day meant we were passed, sometimes a bit too closely for comfort, by lorries and van drivers speeding their way to work.

Eventually, a sign emerged out of the mist saying Annascaul 3 kilometres. The final goal in sight sent surges of energy into us both, and we barely noticed the steady climb from sea level up the hill behind the village.

One more steep descent, some bungalows with illuminated reindeer prancing on their front lawns, and we were there. The village had an unassuming demeanour of a place content to let the world rush by, and it wasn't too difficult to imagine Tom Crean sitting on the stone wall by the bridge with his pipe.

There was no chance of mistaking the pub, with large white letters proudly proclaiming "The South Pole Inn" against its orange walls. Above the porch was a more subtle stone plaque saying "Tom Crean, Antarctic Explorer 1877-1938."

I turned to Nick and said, "We made it!" We indeed had—10:30 a.m., half an hour ahead of plan. The sense of achievement was abruptly replaced by one of complete awe after the lovely lady Tracy, who had worked at the pub for the past eighteen years, let us in and allowed us to roam freely.

Not an inch of wall space was left spare as well-known and less well-known photographs, letters, paintings, news cuttings and artefacts from the heroic age of Antarctic exploration filled every room. In an annexe at the back was a scale replica of the James Caird lifeboat.

The spirit of those great men was tangible as we both sat in silence and looked around, sipping on the best pint of Guinness we'd ever been served. Before we left, we crossed the road to a small public garden, home to a life-sized statue of Tom Crean holding a pair of ski poles and a couple of his beloved pups from the Terra Nova expedition.

I spotted another memorial in this small park: a large irregular rock atop a black marble pillar inscribed "Annascaul to Antarctica." As I touched the rock, I felt an unexpected surge of emotion at the realisation that it had been transported all the way from Grytviken in South Georgia from the actual grave of Sir Ernest Shackleton. It was unveiled in 2015 by Alexandra Shackleton, his granddaughter.

Shackleton died of a heart attack on January 5, 1922, while he was in South Georgia preparing to embark on another Antarctic expedition aboard the ship Quest—the expedition that Crean declined to join.

At the bottom of the monument were the words, "Who is the third who always walks beside you?" This quote is from T.S. Eliot's poem "The Waste Land", inspired by Shackleton's experience during his perilous journey across South Georgia. In his book "South", Shackleton describes feeling the presence of an unseen fourth person.

This phenomenon, called the 'Third Man Factor', refers to the experience of individuals feeling an invisible presence that provides comfort during extreme stress. Examples include Peter Freuchen, an

Arctic explorer, who felt an imaginary companion aiding his survival; the mountaineer Reinhold Messner, during a solo Himalayan climb; Charles Lindbergh, who sensed supportive presences on his transatlantic flight; and astronauts encountering similar phenomena on space missions.

I was more acquainted with a similar phenomenon in Adventure Racing known as 'fifth-person syndrome.' Teams typically consist of four members, but as exhaustion and sleep deprivation set in, we often experience a peculiar confusion: we can only account for three team members and mistakenly believe one is missing. This leads to the sensation that there must be a fifth person and we are constantly searching for them.

On my cycle to the South Pole, I admit I experienced no sensations of an invisible guiding presence; I was too focused on my goal, simultaneously marvelling at the blank canvas of nothingness that spread out in all directions.

The South Pole Inn owner's van featured prominent images of Tom Crean and the Terra Nova, and they graciously offered to drive us to Kerry Airport. We'd booked a one-way rental car to Rosslare for our return overnight ferry. However, we encountered a minor issue: the car rental return was inconveniently located an hour's bike ride north in Wexford, far from the ferry terminal. Fortunately, the rental company demonstrated genuine Irish hospitality by coordinating for us to drop off the car at a B&B across from the ferry, saving us both the trouble and what would have been another hour of pain in the saddle.

It was with a mixture of sadness and satisfaction that we found ourselves back at a dark Rosslare ferry terminal just over one and a half days after we set off. As I had felt at the South Pole ten years earlier, this adventure seemed to be over far too quickly. I didn't feel quite ready to re-enter the fast-paced chaos of daily life: collecting children from school, shopping and tending to an insatiable e-mail inbox...

2023 had been a particularly hard year for many reasons. Wayne and I were going through a separation because we found our differences too hard to bridge. I felt the strain of juggling my Burn Series events business, running the deer park and being a full-time parent. My mother almost died in August from heart failure on the way back from our summer holiday in Sweden. Thankfully, she was saved by the fantastic NHS doctors in not one but three hospitals in Cardiff. It reinforced my belief to make the most of every day and every encounter as if it could be your last.

So, it was with a huge sense of relief and gratitude that I could celebrate Christmas as per our Swedish family tradition at my parents' house in Pembrokeshire with my girls, aged six and eight. My nephew and niece were there, too, and had grown into little adults compared to the ones in the picture I'd carried with me in Antarctica.

In the news, an Italian professional cyclist attempted an Antarctic cycle expedition for the second time by fat bike and seemed to be making slow progress. Once again, the Antarctic season caught up with him, and he had to end his efforts prematurely in January 2024. Things like this cause a part of me to stir, and the unquenchable question enters my mind. "What next?"

At the time of writing, no one has completed a cycle traverse of the Antarctic continent from coast to coast via the South Pole...

Over the past ten years, numerous attempts have been made to cycle to the South Pole and beyond (Appendix 1). Some succeeded, but due to the choice of route and equipment, none could cycle the entire way without towing or pushing their bikes.

It goes without saying that any human-powered expedition to Antarctica requires incredible resilience, planning, and commitment that starts long before setting foot on the continent.

Although the Leverett Glacier route I chose was shorter and better defined, it was an intentional plan to ensure my expedition's best chance of success by cycling every inch of the way to the South Pole. The development of the Polar Cycle and the comprehensive research on Antarctica that it required were intriguing journeys in themselves. My primary goal was to design a vehicle ideally suited for its intended use, utilising the most effective methods informed by current knowledge and insights.

Historical Polar expeditions never intended to make things as difficult as possible; they leveraged every piece of contemporary knowledge and innovation. For example, during my research, I came across a wonderful photograph taken during Shackleton's 1907-1909 Nimrod Expedition showing a modified vintage motor car stuck fast in the ice. This mirrors how I planned my past activities and how I plan to approach all future endeavours.

I maintain contact with Inspired Cycle Engineering, the creators of the original Polar Cycle and was flattered when they requested a high-quality image of my signature to engrave on a special 10th-anniversary edition of their production cycle named the "Full Fat," which is inspired by and generally follows the design of the original.

One evening, I entered the shed that houses my adventure racing and expedition gear collection. The Polar Cycle, a standout piece, is tucked away in a corner. Given the South Wales terrain, it gets little use. On its tenth anniversary, I took the Polar Cycle out for a nostalgic ride across the Merthyr Mawr dunes, the same area where I trained for my Antarctic expedition. Occasionally, the cycle joins me at public speaking events, like a silent partner serving as a physical testament to my journey.

As I stood in the shed, my gaze fell upon the Polar Cycle, now a bit dusty, resting against the vibrant orange of a couple of kayaks. A smile crossed my face as I humorously envisioned a classified ad:

"For Sale: Three-wheel cycle. One careful lady owner. Just one previous journey. Minor tyre wear from ice studs..."

It occurred to me that auctioning off the Polar Cycle and giving the proceeds to charity might be a more noble and generous conclusion. Yet, due to my separation from Wayne, I needed to settle the remaining substantial debts from financing my expedition.

In the future, it might be meaningful to display the Polar Cycle in a museum dedicated to Polar exploration. It could inspire adventure enthusiasts and serve as a beacon for my message: to encourage the enjoyment of sports as a way of life.

# Epilogue

As ten years have passed in what seems more like ten minutes, I feel it's important to look back and consider what has happened over that time. Life goes in waves: up, down, and maybe less frequently than one would like, spells of stillness and calm, much like the sastrugi I had to navigate day after day on the Polar Plateau.

Reflecting on these undulations of the past decade felt particularly relevant as 2024 began, a year promising a surge of opportunities and new goals. Carrying this sense of optimism, I found myself a few weeks after returning from Ireland and my cycle to the South Pole Inn, preparing for a public speaking engagement in London.

The talk was to outline my journey from long before I set foot in Antarctica, touching on the difficult times, the moments of joy, and finally, the realisation that, out of the eight billion people on the planet, I was the first to cycle to the South Pole.

I'd given these talks many times, but something stirred within me on this occasion. I began to challenge the deep-seated belief that I had been on a borrowed path throughout my life. I realised this sentiment was more an inward reflection of my internal feelings about myself than how the outside world perceived me. The audience's positive reactions during the talk and feedback afterwards affirmed this outside view. Clearly, there was some disconnect between the two different perspectives on my story.

Upon reflection, I realised that my journey was not on a borrowed path; my lack of confidence and self-esteem made me doubt my abilities. The origin of the deep-seated feelings I've carried for so long are unclear to me. They might have originated from my school days or perhaps from being accepted into a maths degree course at university despite shockingly bad A-level results. Or the time I was chosen to represent the UK in the Land Rover G4 challenge, even though I couldn't change a tyre during the assessment and was far from the best athlete there. Instances like these planted the seeds of self-doubt. This sense of being an impostor grew when I landed a high-profile job due to a misunderstanding during the job interview. Thrust into this role, I had to learn quickly, adapt, and chart a course through unfamiliar territory. I have only recently started seeing this adaptability as a sign of resourcefulness and strength, not the sense of cheating I once feared.

Luckily, I could demonstrate to those making the decisions that I was worth taking risks with. This was the strength that I should have focused on rather than the negatives.

Nobody is on a borrowed path; everyone has the power to create their own through opportunities, curiosity, connections, timing, and occasionally a bit of good luck. As we navigate each day, we must have complete conviction in these things, even when the going gets tough. The outside world judges based on what we outwardly project, not always accounting for our internal struggles. Finding fulfilment comes from leading a life where our inner selves are closely aligned with the persona we present to the outside world.

The story I shared in my talk in London was a highlight of my ongoing journey. Life has undoubtedly changed since I became a mother to two young girls. Maintaining confidence in being a full-time parent and trying to bolt on as many other things as humanly, sometimes inhumanly possible, has recently become my passionate mission. I use the hypnosis therapy that helped me on my ascent of the Leverett Glacier and later in childbirth to navigate turbulent times.

While reflecting on my path, I've been struck by the broader societal undervaluation of roles including parenthood, which I've learnt intimately. I recently watched a TEDx talk by Marilyn Waring, an advocate for recognising unpaid work in public policy. Marilyn critiques the narrow scope of Gross Domestic Product (GDP) as a measure of a country's economic value, highlighting its failure to account for the substantial contributions of unpaid labour. Her point that GDP classifies the vital activities of giving birth, breastfeeding, stay-at-home parenting, caregiving for the elderly, sick, or disabled, performing household chores, volunteering for community services, and transporting family members to various appointments and activities as 'leisure'—implying they add nothing to society's wealth—both resonated and angered me.

This realisation fuelled a passion to raise awareness about the gross injustice of such economic assessments. It's bewildering how such a perspective is widely accepted, perpetuating inequality and particularly discouraging women from choosing to be stay-at-home parents. The implications are profound: if society fails to value and honour the role of women and stay-at-home parents in nurturing future generations, we risk not only perpetuating gender inequality but also undermining the very fabric of humanity. We must recognise and reward the indispensable roles of volunteering and caregiving to ensure a healthy and equitable future for all.

As a mother, I am responsible for teaching my children everything I know and can do and supporting them in excelling at the activities they love. I have led a very fortunate life and am so lucky to have so many stories and experiences from near and far that I can share with them. This includes all the lessons and coping mechanisms required to navigate the modern world, such as the invisible circle.

Every day is an adventure, and I hope reading my stories inspires you to embrace and celebrate the unique path you forge.

The timeless wisdom of the Roman Emperor Marcus Aurelius struck a chord with me: "The impediment to action becomes the action. What stands in the way becomes the way." This philosophy has guided me through letting go of the past and embracing the unknown, leading to a transformation in every aspect of my existence.

In Swedish, we have the word 'dörrtröskelmilen'—the 'doorstep mile'—which conveys the concept of overcoming the initial resistance to stepping outside and beginning an adventure. It's this concept that I'd like to extend to all readers, whether or not you have an affinity for sports or outdoor pursuits. What begins as a single step outside your comfort zone can transform into a monumental stride, revealing your true self to the world. I invite you to take that step, find growth in the challenges, and let your story unfold.

# Acknowledgements

I sincerely thank my parents, Adrianne and Anders Leijerstam, whose love, inspiration, and unwavering support have shaped me into who I am today. I cannot thank you enough for everything.

To Nick Russill, my soulmate, your historical expertise and eloquence have greatly enriched this second edition. Thank you also for accompanying me on the 300-kilometre cycle through the wind and rain in Ireland to the South Pole Inn.

Wayne Edy, thank you for all your support and the sacrifices you made in accompanying me and believing in me when so few others did.

A special thanks to Chris Parker at Inspired Cycle Engineering (ICE) for taking my wild expedition idea and, with limited time and notice, turning it into something extraordinary. The cycle was indeed perfect for the job.

I am very grateful to Marcus Eales and Chris Davies at Qoroz Titanium Bikes for their faith in me and for helping to form the foundation of the expedition. I do love a good titanium bike!

Emil and Torfi at Arctic Trucks have been patient, unassuming, and supportive, allowing me the space to make critical decisions. Together, we embarked on quite the adventure.

Ryan Edy, thank you for your incredible photographs in Iceland that captured the essence of the training.

My thanks to Rob Taylor at Tamworth Snowdome for not only giving us access to your facility but also for the unexpected post-adventure task of sending back the wheels I left behind. Your generosity has not gone unnoticed.

The Gatorade Sports Science Institute at Loughborough University, specifically Dr. James Carter and Rebecca Randall, provided invaluable advice. Seeing the results on paper was pivotal in sharpening my focus.

Tony Markland at Ferryspeed, cycling my Polar Cycle around your frozen warehouse was an unusual sight for your staff, but it created the perfect training environment. I am deeply thankful for that.

I'd also like to acknowledge the National Maritime Museum and the Captain Scott Society.

Alex Lloyd Jenkins deserves a special mention for creating the cover artwork for this second edition.

Heartfelt thanks go to Mountain Equipment, Haglofs, INOV8, Vitabiotics, Bikemongers, Powertraveller, Bloc, Yaesu, Best Grip, I.D, Yellowbrick, Cotswold, Attivastudio, St David's Hotel & Spa, Apidura, and 9-Bar for their support.

I must extend my warmest appreciation of Irish hospitality, particularly to the landlord and landlady of Fitzgerald's Pub in Ballymagooly and Gary and Tracy at the South Pole Inn in Annascaul.

Finally, this book is indebted to the heroic individuals who, throughout history, overcame tremendous challenges to reveal Antarctica's secrets. Their courage set the stage for today's advancements in comprehending this captivating wilderness. Their legacy of perseverance and innovation inspires ongoing exploration and conservation, highlighting Antarctica's significance for environmental awareness and the beauty of our planet.

# Author's Note

I am incredibly grateful you've accompanied me on my journey; your presence as a reader has been invaluable. The experiences and memories captured within these pages are dear to my heart, and I hope they have also resonated with you.

To enhance your experience, I have curated an online gallery featuring high-resolution images to accompany this book. These photographs bring to life the adventures and landscapes described in the book. To access this exclusive content, scan the QR code below or visit:

www.marialeijerstam.com/sp2013gallery

Your feedback is crucial to me. If this book has touched you or sparked your sense of adventure, I would be extremely grateful if you could share your impressions. Posting your review on Amazon and spreading the word among your friends and through your social media channels helps to support my work and connect with other readers who might enjoy this journey as much as you have.

# Appendix 1

## ANTARCTIC EXPEDITIONS INVOLVING CYCLING

### 1911: Captain Scott's Terra Nova Expedition
Thomas Griffith Taylor (British)
Distance Travelled: ~15 miles (~25 km)
Taylor travelled on a regular bicycle to the tongue of the Mount Erebus Glacier as part of a geological and geomorphological survey. Exhausted, he had to carry the bike back on foot.

### 2003 Patriot Hills Bike Expedition
### Doug Stoup (American)
Distance travelled: 200 miles (320 km)
The explorer and guide led the first bike expedition in Antarctica in January 2003, traversing around Patriot Hills on a custom "ice bike."

### 2012 Kite, Ski and Bike Expedition
### Helen Skelton (British)
Distance travelled: 500 miles (805 km)
A BBC television project that eventually reached the South Pole after completing a multi-disciplinary journey, partially cycling with a custom-built bike with 8-inch tyres, pulling a sledge with supplies.

### 2012 Attempt to Cycle to the South Pole
### Eric Larsen (American)
Distance travelled: 335 miles (539 km)
He attempted a solo bicycle ride from Hercules Inlet with food drops from the coast to the South Pole. He was forced to abandon after cycling roughly a quarter of the way to the South Pole, having pedalled 175 miles (282 km) on a fat bike.

### 2013 First Successful Cycle to the South Pole
### & Fastest Human-Powered Journey
### Maria Leijerstam (British)
Distance travelled: 396 miles (637 km)
Maria set two world records with her custom-designed Polar Cycle.
She cycled every meter from the edge of the Antarctic continent to
the South Pole, starting on the Ross Ice Shelf via the Leverett Glacier.
She also set the human-powered speed record in just 10 days, 14
hours, and 56 minutes. She was partially supported.

### 2013-2014 Cycle & Ski to the South Pole
### Juan Menéndez Granados (Spanish)
Distance travelled: 775 miles (1,247 km)
He embarked on a solo, unsupported, and unassisted bicycle and ski
expedition to the South Pole from Hercules Inlet and finished on
January 17, 2014, after 46 days.

### 2013 Team Ski & Cycle to the South Pole
### Australian 3-man team
Distance travelled: 385 miles (620 km)
Keith Tuffley, Eric Phillips and Robert Smith cycled, skied and
pushed to the South Pole via the Reedy Glacier.

### 2013-2014 Cycle to the South Pole
### Daniel P. Burton (American)
Distance travelled: 775 miles (1,247 km)
A bicycle expedition to the South Pole starting at Hercules Inlet on a
Fat bike. When cycling was not feasible, he pushed his bike. His
expedition included pre-arranged food caches and one equipment
cache. He finished on January 21, 2014, after 51 days.

### 2022 Attempt to Cycle to the South Pole
### Omar Di Felice (Italian)
Distance travelled: 59 miles (95 km)
A cycle attempt from Hercules Inlet to the South Pole. He was forced
to abandon his expedition after eight days and 59 miles (95 km).

## 2023: Attempt to Cycle to the South Pole
## Omar Di Felice (Italian)
Distance travelled: 445 miles (716 km)
He returned for a second attempt but stopped at Thiels Corner (85°05' S on the Hercules Inlet - South Pole track) after 48 days and 445 miles (716.5 km), again on a fat bike.

# Appendix 2

## SPECIFICATION OF THE POLAR CYCLE

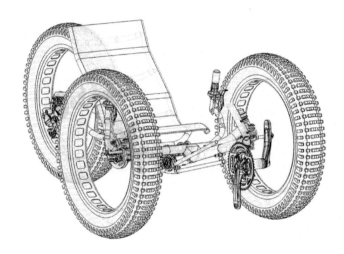

**Gearing**

1. 27-speed gear system
2. Front chainrings: 22-32-44 tooth Oval chainrings, custom-made by Inspired Cycle Engineering Ltd. (ICE), optimal for hill climbing and ultra-distance cycling
3. Mid-drive with a 2:1 step-down ratio, effectively halving the gear ratio for easier pedalling on steep terrain
4. Rear cassette: 9-speed 12-36 sprockets, standard MTB configuration known for durability
5. Gear shifters: Bar end type, designed for easy operation with large gloves
6. Chain: YBN Heavy-duty, composed of three standard chains linked together
7. Expected speed range: 2 to 12 mph while pedalling at a comfortable cadence of 60-75 rpm

## Wheels
1. Hubs: Hope FatSno, specially reinforced "super tough" rear hub designed to withstand high loads and forces from low gearing, manufactured in Britain
2. Rims: Surly Clown Shoe, 100mm wide
3. Rear tyre: Surly Lou 4.8", the largest and most aggressive tyre available at the time, fitted with ice studs for enhanced traction
4. Front tyres: Surly Big Fat Larry, chosen for being the largest, most comfortable, and best for steering
5. Wheel construction: All wheels were hand-built by ICE

## Brakes
Standard MTB disc brakes (cable-operated, not hydraulic).

## Frame
1. Material: 4130 Cro-Mo (Chromoly) aircraft-grade steel
2. Purpose: Engineered for total reliability in extreme environments
3. Construction: Hand-built by ICE (Inspired Cycle Engineering)
4. Bespoke luggage rack designed by ICE to carry up to 80kg

## Seat
Standard ICE seat with added "Love Handles" to keep Maria in place over uneven ground.

## Pedals
Custom built by ICE to accommodate Maria's polar boots.

www.marialeijerstam.com

Printed in Great Britain
by Amazon

41393159R00116